MAYWOOD PUBLIC LIBRARY

W9-BUB-988

MAYWOOD PUBLIC LIBRARY
121 SOUTH 5TH AVE.
MAYWOOD, ILL. 60153

THE ULTIMATE
DOLL BOOK

THE ULTIMATE
DOLL BOOK

Caroline Goodfellow

Foreword by
Dorothy and Evelyn Jane Coleman

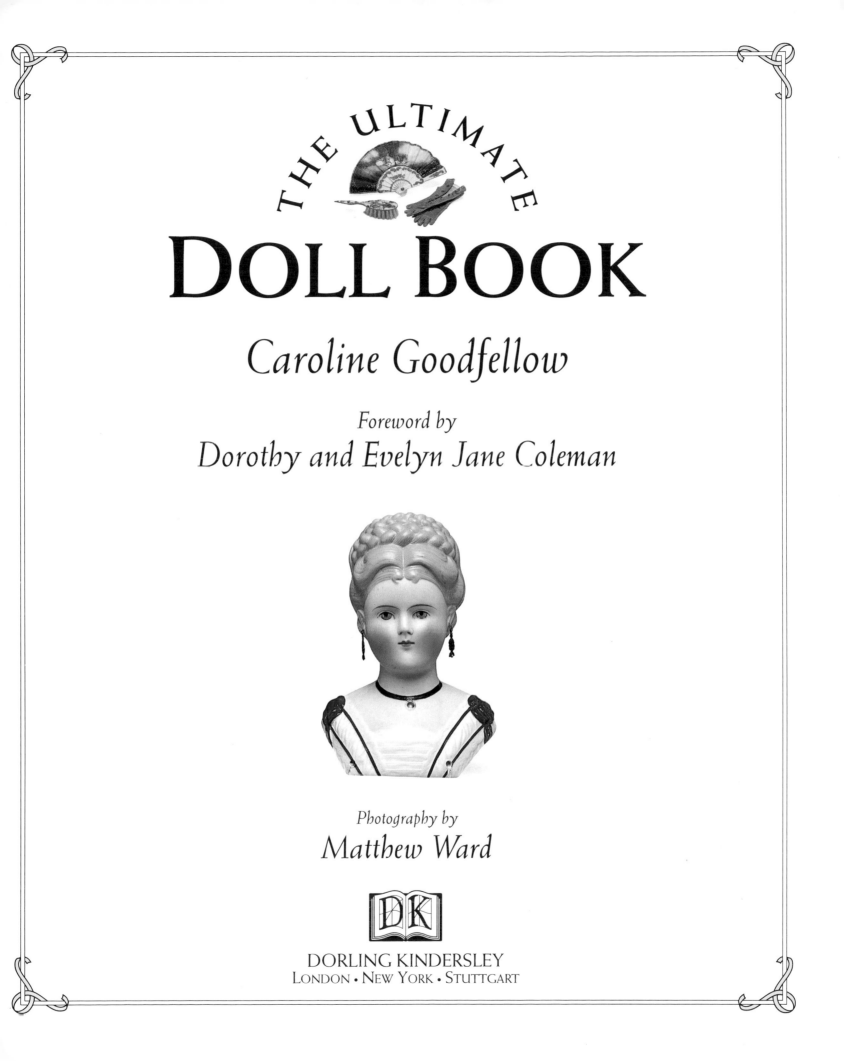

Photography by
Matthew Ward

DK

DORLING KINDERSLEY
LONDON · NEW YORK · STUTTGART

A DORLING KINDERSLEY BOOK

Project Editor Gillian Roberts
Art Editor Kevin Ryan
Assisting Editor Polly Boyd
Production Meryl Silbert
Managing Editor Mary-Clare Jerram
Managing Art Editor Gill Della Casa
Consultant Faith Eaton
US Editor Laaren Brown

First American Edition, 1993
2 4 6 8 10 9 7 5 3 1
Published in the United States by
Dorling Kindersley, Inc., 232 Madison Avenue
New York, New York 10016

Copyright © 1993
Dorling Kindersley Limited, London
Text copyright © 1993 Caroline Goodfellow

All rights reserved under International and Pan-American
Copyright Conventions. No part of this publication may
be reproduced, stored in a retrieval system, or transmitted in
any form or by any means, electronic, mechanical, photocopying,
recording, or otherwise, without the prior written
permission of the copyright owners. Published in Great Britain
by Dorling Kindersley Limited.
Distributed by Houghton Mifflin Company, Boston.

Library of Congress Cataloging-in-Publication Data

Goodfellow, Caroline G. (Caroline Georgina)
The ultimate doll book / by Caroline Goodfellow: foreword by
Dorothy and Evelyn Jane Coleman -- 1st American ed.

p. cm.
Includes index.
ISBN 1-56458-273-6
1. Dolls--History. I. Title.

NK4894.A2G66 1993

688.7'221'09--dc20 92-30516
CIP

Computer page makeup by
Cooling Brown Partnership, Great Britain

Text film output by
The Right Type, Great Britain

Reproduced by Colourscan, Singapore

Printed and bound in Great Britain by Butler and Tanner

Descriptions of the dolls on these pages can be
found in the appropriate sections of the book.
On page 1: *"Solid Comfort"* (*see p. 88*). On page 2:
"Old Pretender" (*see p. 13*). On page 3: *Patterned
Shoulder Head* (*see p. 49*). On page 4: *"Harry the
Hawk"* (*see p. 103*). On page 5 top: *Mandarin with
Long Fingers* (*see p. 135*).

Contents

PORCELAIN PARADE (*BELOW*) *This selection of nine bisque and untinted bisque dolls illustrates the fine craftsmanship of French and German doll-makers in the late 19th and early 20th centuries.*

Foreword

Dorothy and Evelyn Jane Coleman

GLAZED CHINA DOLL
(BELOW) This fine example from the Coleman Collection was made in Germany between 1865 and 1870, and has the typically classical look that was so fashionable at that time. The shoulder plate has a molded, decorated design. The body is of stuffed cloth, with kid lower arms. Ht: 20in (50cm)

EVEN IN THE DAYS of the early Greeks, dolls were part of domestic life, and since then they have played a significant role in almost every civilization. Today, collecting dolls is a prominent, popular pursuit worldwide: everywhere, dolls are objects of great interest and desirability.

∽ It has been our good fortune to visit numerous museums and private collections of dolls throughout the world. What a thrill it is to see the early native dolls in Alaska, the many dolls of the Americas, the Australian dolls, and of course, the dolls in Europe. Recently, we revisited Thuringia, in Germany, where the majority of the dolls in our collection were originally produced. Sadly, its once-prosperous doll-making industry has almost ceased to exist, but the antique dolls themselves live on in public displays and individual collections.

Looking at Dolls

In 1992, during our second visit to Australia, we gave many talks on dolls, including a program of lectures at the Powerhouse Museum in Sydney. Some of the people attending had traveled long distances just to be there. While we were at the museum, the curator showed some of the dolls that had been brought to Australia in the distant past. Most had never before been seen by the public, and not even by doll collectors in Australia. We were not certain which gave them the greater pleasure: was it the very special privilege of seeing these dolls that had come to Australia long ago, or the rare opportunity of viewing our color slides of different and exciting dolls from around the world?

∽ Fortunately, one does not always have to travel a great distance in order to see pictures of beautiful dolls. Readers of *The Ultimate Doll Book* can look at, study, and enjoy some of the dolls that belong to

"LADY BETTY MODISH"
(ABOVE) This elegant, c. 1902 Kestner bisque-headed doll (see pages 74–75) is one of the major exhibits at the Wenham Museum. Ht: 17½in (45cm)

major private collections such as Faith Eaton's, in England, and our own, in the United States: both of these have been decades in the making. *The Ultimate Doll Book* also provides wonderful photographs of dolls from London's Bethnal Green Museum of Childhood (a branch of the Victoria & Albert Museum) and in the United States, the Wenham Historical Association and Museum, in Massachusetts. These two museums have outstanding collections of dolls; some of the dolls date back many years, or even centuries.

The World of the Collector

Once you buy a doll, hopefully you will live with it for many years; as you learn more about it, your doll may become an even greater treasure. Seek dolls in as original condition as possible, not ones that have been repaired or altered. Be sure the clothes are of about the same period as the doll, too. Examine and familiarize yourself with the marks and every detail of their heads, bodies, and clothes, especially the shoes. This can tell you a considerable amount about your dolls, such as who made them and where – and perhaps, when – they were made.

Frauds and Fakes

Dolls are often put together at various stages of their lives. For example, the head could be purchased and the rest of the doll made at home; parts may have been replaced at a doll hospital; or dealers today can put parts of different ages together to create a doll. If a doll that appeals to you has been altered and wears recently made clothes, wait until you can find a similar doll, but in its original condition, including the wig and the costume.

Future Preservation

Millions and millions of dolls with bisque heads were made in the nineteenth and early twentieth centuries, yet only a few have survived intact. Their modern, porcelain relatives – now often produced as collectors' dolls rather than toys – do not have to suffer the same harsh treatment. They are handled with care, so that they will be available for years to come. Now, many of the dolls of old are being given similar consideration. At least a few surviving old dolls, as well as some newer ones, can be enjoyed in *The Ultimate Doll Book*, and thus provide pleasure for this and future generations.

WAX-OVER-COMPOSITION (ABOVE) *Made in the mid-19th century in England or Germany, this doll from the Faith Eaton Collection has a wax-over-papier-mâché shoulder head, cloth body and upper arms and legs, and kid lower arms. Ht: 31in (80cm)*

WATERCOLOR MINIATURE (ABOVE) *One of a group of miniatures, "The Four Whitmore Children," by 18th-century artist Paul-Peter Lens shows a girl holding a contemporary doll.*

PIEROTTI DOLL (BELOW) *Made by Pierotti in England in the early 20th century, this lady is exhibited at the Bethnal Green Museum of Childhood. It has a poured wax shoulder head and lower arms and legs. The skill of the maker is evident in the fine modeling and graceful pose of the doll's hands. Ht: 16in (41cm)*

Introducing Dolls

ASK TEN DIFFERENT PEOPLE "What is a doll?" and you will probably get as many different answers, each one qualified by the period, culture, and society that have formed and shaped that person's singular perception of the world. Yet, crossing all barriers of individual perspective and time, race, and class, we discover the generally accepted idea of what a doll is: an inanimate object that represents a human being in miniature.

In *The Ultimate Doll Book*, we have chosen to focus on dolls intended for use as playthings. Of course, there are many other types of dolls: dolls' house dolls and paper dolls, marionettes and puppets, to name just a few. All these are quite separate subjects in their own right. Vying for attention with the play dolls featured in this book, they would not have received the closely detailed pictorial and textual commentary they deserve.

Although all the dolls illustrated and described in these pages were made within the past 300 years, our knowledge of ancient civilizations leads us directly to the assumption that dolls did not suddenly appear in the seventeenth century but had evolved to that point over thousands of years. A swift trip through *The Ultimate Doll Book* reveals a continuing ebb and flow to this process of gradual evolution, as new materials and innovative manufacturing techniques have changed the course of doll-making history.

GIRL WITH A DOLL
(ABOVE) This oil-on-canvas painting, entitled "Portrait of Lilly, Daughter of J. Noble, Esq.," is the work of English artist Sir John Everett Millais, who lived between 1826 and 1896. The figure held by the child shows an example of the gorgeously dressed lady dolls that were made in France in the later years of this period.

C.1915 CHARCOAL SELLER *(BELOW) Created in the United States by one of the Vargus family of New Orleans, this wax doll represents a "Cry" of the city. Cries, which portray familiar trades and occupations, usually take the form of pictures rather than three-dimensional objects. Ht: 7in (18cm)*

Dolls as Playthings

The use to which dolls have been put over the years has varied enormously, from religious offerings at one end of the spectrum to playthings at the other. But the majority of the dolls produced between 1680 and the 1990s – the time period covered by our book – were almost certainly intended to be used as children's playthings. Many were designed for a particular age group: in the eighteenth century, simple rag dolls, stitched and stuffed by mothers using any readily available household materials, were generally made as comfort toys for young babies and children under five.

In England, older middle-class children had "Sunday only" dolls, which were taken out to be played with under strict adult supervision for an hour or two in the afternoon. The elegantly attired, bisque-headed fashion dolls and those with elaborately molded hairstyles, made in France and Germany in the latter half of the nineteenth century, fall into this category.

∾ Since the 1930s, more and more dolls have been mass-produced, particularly in the United States. Faced with rising costs and the whims of a must-have buying public, manufacturers target niche markets as a matter of survival, ensuring a good return on their capital outlay and investment.

Chronology and Order

The ten sections of *The Ultimate Doll Book* are arranged so that the materials from which dolls have been made are described as they were first used for this purpose, in a loosely knit chronology. History is not so neatly ordered, however, that one section begins where the previous section came to an end: doll-makers did not stop using one material simply because another became available.

∾ Some materials, such as wood, have stepped backward in their "evolution." Others, for example bisque, have been superseded by newer ones. Even within the bounds of this scenario, a material can be rediscovered, perhaps in a novel form. Individual doll-makers are now using a ceramic-like art clay called Sculpey, formulated in the United States, to create doll heads with the look of fine bisque porcelain.

∾ Manufacturing innovations have played their part in the story as well. Realistically modeled plastic dolls would scarcely be possible without the techniques of injection molding that were developed in the 1940s. For some, such technology allows realism to be carried to unpalatable extremes: Villy Nielsen's Judith "Mother and Baby" – a doll with a spring-loaded abdominal cavity that "gives birth" to a tiny baby – and Effe's male-sexed *Bimbovero* are not to everyone's taste.

The Language of Dolls

Remember, as you read *The Ultimate Doll Book*, that unfamiliar words, or familiar words used in unfamiliar ways, are just a means of identifying the different types of dolls. Transported into nineteenth-century France, "doll" becomes *bébé* (baby) for dolls representing young children as well as babies, and *poupée* (doll) for older child and adult dolls – confusing stuff for newcomers who might assume that a French *bébé Jumeau* is a Jumeau baby doll. But learning the special language of dolls is all part of the fun of discovering this fascinating subject.

VOGUE DOLLS, GINNY
(ABOVE) *Hard plastic was a popular doll-making material after World War II. Wearing the uniform of the Girl Scouts of America, this model was made by Vogue Dolls, Inc., between 1957 and 1962. Ht: 7in (18cm)*

RUSSIAN NESTING DOLL, YELTSIN (BELOW) *The correct term for these brightly painted wooden dolls is matryoshka. The dolls fit inside one another and are usually made in series of between six and ten figures. Ht: 4¼in (11cm)*

BÉBÉ JUMEAU (ABOVE) *Large, bulbous eyes are a feature of early Jumeau dolls. This one is described in extensive detail on page 58. Doll ht: 22in (55cm)*

1980S GERMAN DOLL (BELOW) *The original wrist tag bears the legend "Stupsi, your lovable cuddly companion." A bendable soft vinyl doll, Stupsi has a soft and cozy covering of stockinette. Ht: 17in (43cm)*

Wooden Dolls

Inexpensive and readily available, wood has always been used for making dolls. Wooden dolls with any accurately documented history date from c.1680, although they were, of course, made before this time. A few figures have been found in ancient burial sites, yet genuine examples of very early dolls have all but disappeared — destroyed, perhaps as idolatrous images during times of religious conflict, or simply deemed not worth keeping.

RECORDS DOCUMENTING DOLL-MAKING activities show that of the dolls surviving from the 1600s and 1700s, the majority – or even all – are English. Most are made of pine, a wood that was in plentiful supply, easy to carve or turn on a lathe, but also able to withstand rough treatment. As with other types of doll, a great number of wooden dolls were made by parents for their children, but the most

LADY AND LORD CLAPHAM (*LEFT and RIGHT*) *These two carved wooden dolls wear "Fashionable Undress" – costumes so typical of the late 17th-century English upper class that they date the pair c.1690. The similarity between the dolls suggests that they are probably the work of a single maker. Both are fully painted over a gesso base and have painted eyes and facial features. Ht: 19in (48cm)*

accomplished examples are almost certainly the work of professional carvers, making dolls for sale.

∽ In Europe, the toy-making industry (which also produced dolls) evolved over more than two hundred years. By the 1600s, it was established as an organized craft guild alongside other guilds that embraced similarly traditional skills. This indicates that doll-making existed in Europe long before the end of the eighteenth century, when dolls attributed to European makers came onto the market. In the Grödener Tal region of Austria (now a part of Italy) and in Oberammergau, Berchtesgaden, and Sonneberg, three small German towns, rich forests of pine provided abundant raw materials for making dolls. The town of Erzgebirge, near Dresden, was another energetic wooden toy-making center.

Early Dolls

The early wooden dolls – those made between 1680 and 1720 – are considered to be carefully crafted. Each has the head and torso carved as one, and shows a distinctly individual facial expression, with painted or inset glass eyes, and noses, mouths, and ears which are well defined. Their limbs are attached by various pinning and jointing methods, according to the material. The upper arms are most usually made of bound

PEG WOODENS POSTCARD
(*RIGHT*) *During the 1890s, Bertha Upton wrote a series of children's books, illustrated by her daughter, Florence. The series inspired a line of merchandise, including card games and postcards. The adventures of two peg wooden dolls (and their friend, Golliwogg) were some of their most popular stories.*

GRÖDENER TAL SHOULDER HEADS
(*ABOVE and RIGHT*) *Sometimes known as Wooden Bettys, and now rather rare, heads such as these inexpensive 1930s designs were mass-produced from 1880 to 1940, mainly for export. They are crudely carved and painted, and are usually attached to coarse cloth bodies. Ht: 4in (10cm)*

linen, while the lower parts are made of carved wood. Fingers and thumbs are separate and many examples display fingernail detail. Wood was usually used for the upper and lower legs. The feet tend to be skillfully made, with well-carved toes and toenails. The whole body was covered with a base layer of gesso first, then delicately painted, and finally varnished. The finished dolls were dressed in stylish costumes of the period.

A Retrograde Development

After 1720, wooden dolls deteriorated rather than improving in quality. A more stylized, less individual appearance is conveyed in the dolls' flattened faces

and facial features. The painstaking carving of the earlier doll bodies gave way to a roughly fashioned torso and limbs, although the narrow-waisted, broad-hipped shape was retained. As before, the wooden limbs and knee joints were attached to the torso with pegged tongue and groove joints. When all-wooden arms had replaced the earlier linen-and-wooden type, tongue and groove joints were also applied to the shoulders and elbows. Despite the relatively unrefined workmanship, the joints themselves are surprisingly efficient, allowing easy mobility for the arms and legs. Ball joints were used for some 1800s dolls, giving them the look of an artist's mannequin or lay figure, and providing their limbs with even greater freedom of movement than the tongue and groove joints.

Finishing techniques were also less sophisticated than those of earlier dolls. The gesso base layer was still used, but paint was applied only to the face and upper torso – areas that were meant to resemble naked "flesh" – while the rest of the body was left white. Toward the end of the 1700s, even the gesso layer was abandoned, and doll bodies were unpainted, showing the bare wood.

The overall decline in the quality of wooden dolls continued into the nineteenth and twentieth centuries. They were generally considered throwaway items, and their appearance only helped to support this view. However, once again, some of the dolls did exhibit the individual personality of the 1680s dolls, as we can observe in the work of such fine craftsmen as the innovative American doll-makers Joel Ellis (see page 14) and Albert Schoenhut (see page 15).

LUCKY MASCOT (*LEFT*) *Small wooden dolls were once peddled at the Derby – a classic fixture of the English racing season – and worn in the hatband for good luck. Sir John Everett Millais's pen and ink drawing of 1853 pokes fun at a couple's despair after losing a bet.*

Early Dolls

· 1680s to 1820s ·

MOST EARLY WOODEN DOLLS were made in England, probably in and around London, by a number of different makers. Fewer than 30 seventeenth-century English wooden dolls have survived. Female dolls far outnumber males, which have the same shape, but are dressed in masculine attire. The formal appearance and fashionable clothing of both types suggests that they were made for adults, rather than as children's playthings.

Dolls of this period are often called "Queen Anne" dolls – a misnomer, because most were made either before 1702 or after 1714, the years of her reign. Dating these rare, virtually priceless dolls is difficult. The clothes, usually sewn to the body, do not allow examination of the naked figure, which would reveal clues to the doll's age.

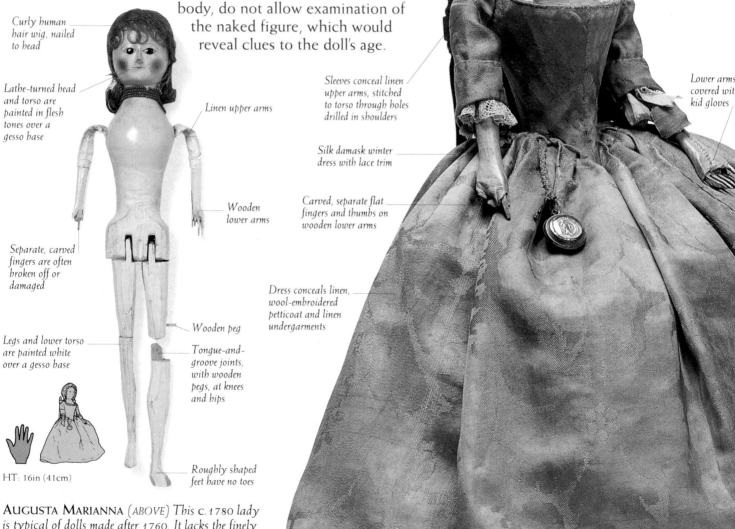

Curly human hair wig, nailed to head

Lathe-turned head and torso are painted in flesh tones over a gesso base

Linen upper arms

Wooden lower arms

Separate, carved fingers are often broken off or damaged

Wooden peg

Tongue-and-groove joints, with wooden pegs, at knees and hips

Legs and lower torso are painted white over a gesso base

Roughly shaped feet have no toes

HT: 16in (41cm)

Head and torso made from one block of wood, turned on a lathe and carved

Dark brown glass eyes, embedded in slots cut in the face

Torso has a rounded chest, narrow waist, flat back, and broad, squarish hips

Sleeves conceal linen upper arms, stitched to torso through holes drilled in shoulders

Lower arms are covered with kid gloves

Silk damask winter dress with lace trim

Carved, separate flat fingers and thumbs on wooden lower arms

Dress conceals linen, wool-embroidered petticoat and linen undergarments

AUGUSTA MARIANNA (ABOVE) This c.1780 lady is typical of dolls made after 1760. It lacks the finely modeled features of earlier dolls, an example of which can be seen on the right. Ht: 19in (48cm)

1745 DOLL (RIGHT) The well-defined nose, mouth, lozenge-shaped eyes, and brows and lashes (indicated with dots of paint) give this figure a definite personality.

Bulbous glass eyes, slotted into face

Head and narrow-waisted torso carved from one piece of wood

Well-defined nose, ears, and mouth

Shaped and painted breasts

Finely carved hands show rounded fingers with fingernails

Original linen upper arms have been rebound and nailed to the shoulders

Carved, but not separate, toes

Hips are carved on each side to house tongues from leg joints

Wide-hipped lower torso, shaped at back to suggest buttocks

Lower legs have fine calves and ankles

UNCLOTHED MODEL (ABOVE) This doll, made between 1700 and 1720, is remarkable in its relatively close resemblance to the human form. Its unclothed state provides a rare opportunity to study the maker's craftsmanship. Ht: 19in (48cm)

"FASHIONABLE UNDRESS FOR SPRING 1755" (RIGHT) In the mid-1700s, a young English girl, Laetitia Clark Powell, created doll costumes based on dresses she had once worn herself. This costume, made when she was 13, is worn by a typical, stylized wooden doll. Ht: 11in (28cm)

Cloth covers wooden lower arms, to look like gloves

Human hair wig

Brown glass eyes

Painted facial features

Informal "at-home" costume made of silk brocade

EUROPEAN RIVAL, C.1820 (RIGHT) From the end of the 18th century, cheaper German dolls competed with the expensive English models. They were painted directly onto the wood, on areas that would show: the costly gesso base layer was entirely omitted. Ht: 8½in (22cm)

Painted hair, eyes, and mouth

Wedge, inserted into face, forms nose

Limbs are attached to torso with wooden pegs

1680s carved walnut and cane chair, styled after full-sized chairs in Holyroodhouse

Head and body, carved from separate pieces of wood, are gessoed and painted

Painted eyes, a feature of many early dolls

Black beauty patches were the height of fashion

Kid-covered hands appear large, but are in proportion to head

"OLD PRETENDER" (ABOVE) The attire, face patches, and known history of this doll suggest it was made c.1680. It is said that it belonged to the court of King James II at Holyroodhouse in Edinburgh, Scotland. Ht: 21in (53cm)

Dolls from the New World

· 1850s to 1930s ·

IN THE UNITED STATES, New England was the creative center for toy- and doll-making in the mid-nineteenth century. Many American makers were by this time already established producers of wooden toys, but their doll designs, though innovative, were often unsuccessful: the buying public, composed largely of recently settled Europeans, found dolls of the familiar European style and type more to its taste (see pages 18–19). Some early American dolls were the work of individuals, made in their spare time; other makers progressed to form companies that manufactured dolls on a grander scale. By the twentieth century, makers were often immigrants who had worked with toys or dolls in their native land, and the making of dolls had spread beyond New England to many other parts of the country.

Hair is usually brownish black; blond hair is rare

Molded facial features are hand-painted

Dowel rod attaches rigid head to body

Head and neck are painted to resemble skin

Mortise and tenon joints at shoulders give full articulation

Upper torso is painted yellow

Mortise and tenon joints at elbows

Stiffened cotton apron, with printed "embroidery" in a traditional design

Mortise and tenon joints at hips

Hands and wrists are made of cast lead, painted cream

A metal pin secures each mortise and tenon joint

Flesh-toned paint on lower legs

Cast lead feet and ankles, painted to resemble boots

Hand-painted drawstring purse, tied to wrist

Bloomers trimmed with intricate cotton tatting

JOEL ELLIS, 1873 PATENTED DOLL The Co-operative Manufacturing Co. produced these dolls for the Vermont Novelty Works, founded in 1858 by Joel Ellis, Rodney Britton, and Ellis Eaton in Springfield, Massachusetts. Ellis's doll has a rock maple head, steamed and shaped in a hydraulic press, and lead hands and feet.

HT: 15in (38cm)

KENTUCKY MOUNTAIN PAIR

(RIGHT) Dating from the 1930s, this pair is thought to be the work of one person making dolls as a hobby, rather than a company. The male figure is distinguished from the female essentially by its clothes, and in small details such as the hair and body padding. Ht: 10in (25cm)

Brown, poor-quality mohair wig, stuck to head

Solid wood head, with crudely carved facial features

Cheeks and chin are stained with pink ink or water-based paint

Cloth-over-wood padded upper torso

Wooden lower and upper arms

Suit conceals stuffed cloth upper legs and lower torso

Wooden lower legs, with blue ink- or paint-stained feet

Eyes, lashes, and brows are defined with pencil

Female figure has no padding

Both dolls have a handwritten ink mark on the upper back that reads "Hall," probably the name of the maker.

SCHOENHUT ALL-WOOD PERFECTION ART DOLL

(BELOW) Albert Schoenhut, a German immigrant, started trading in Philadelphia, Pennsylvania, in 1872. In 1911, his company was awarded a patent for an all-wood doll with metal spring joints. The unique flexible jointing system allows much movement, but is rigid enough for the doll to be posed without falling over. Ht: 16in (40cm)

Solid wood head

Hair is molded with the head and painted yellowish blond

Head turns a full 360°

Mortise and tenon joints, with wooden pegs, at shoulders and hips

Rock maple body, unpainted on parts likely to be clothed

Ball and socket joints at knees and elbows

Cast lead feet, painted blue to represent boots

Dress conceals feet, which are almost identical to the man's

Joints at elbows, neck, shoulders, wrists, hips, knees, and ankles

The mark is pressed into the upper back of the doll. This model was made until 1939.

JOINTED DOLL COMPANY

(LEFT) This doll has ball and socket joints patented by George W. Sanders, and a composition-over-wood head, patented by Charles C. Johnson. It was produced and distributed by the Jointed Doll Co., Springfield, Vermont, c. 1880. Ht: 12in (30cm)

Oblique hole allows doll to hold foot in tiptoe position

Straight hole allows doll to hold the foot resting flat

Poupards and Simple Dolls

· 1800s to the present day ·

NOT ALL OF THE EARLIEST DOLLS were as sophisticated as the elegant individuals shown on pages 12 and 13. Stump dolls (simple, one-piece figures, carved from a block of wood) were produced during the same period in England and Germany. The majority were quite roughly made, although some had intricate painted decoration that showed the type of clothing worn by fashionable ladies.

Poupards succeeded stump dolls and came mainly from the Erzgebirge region of Germany. These legless (arms were an occasional feature) figures were crudely carved or turned on a lathe, then painted in bright colors. Poupards usually represent babies in swaddling clothes, or men and women. Twentieth-century versions sometimes have the added refinement of jointed heads and arms or sound mechanisms. Other types of simple dolls are those made from wooden spoons or old-fashioned straight clothespins, materials that remain firm favorites with makers even today.

Carved grooves give texture to painted hair

Nose is a triangular wedge of wood, inserted into a slit in the face

Crudely painted mouth

Painted hair continues around back of doll's head

Painted wavy line around neck, suggesting lace trim on the swaddling

Doll's name and origin, handwritten in pencil in German script, "Thÿmiane/die Düftende/geboren zu/Sterzing/20. Juli 1926" (Thÿmiane/the Aromatic One/born in/Sterzing/20 July 1926)

Doll is roughly carved from one piece of wood, with smoother finish on head and torso

Painted floral decoration is applied over the body base color

Flat back has been left unpainted

Lower part of inscription is illegible

THE "AROMATIC ONE" *Thÿmiane die Düftende is the female half of a pair of large poupards. According to the pencil inscriptions on their backs, the doll and its male companion, the "Awkward One" – Schnattissimo der Rüpel – were "born" in the German village of Sterzing on July 20th, 1926. Both figures are painted, on the front only, to represent young babies swaddled, or wrapped, in cloth strips, in the traditional fashion.*

Front of figure is painted with flesh tones, now faded to cream

HT: 11in (28cm)

Face and upper torso are painted in flesh tones

Unjointed wooden arms, pegged to torso at shoulders

Painted lower arms are unvarnished

Legs end in roughly shaped painted shoes

1920s PEG WOODEN (ABOVE)
Large numbers of cheap dolls were produced in Grödener Tal throughout the 1800s. The 20th-century version shown here differs from them only in its "flapper" costume. Ht: 6in (15cm)

WOMAN WITH HAT (BELOW)
Poupards with arms usually represent adults. This German doll was made between 1900 and 1930, but is based on an old design. Ht: 6in (15cm)

Arms, carved as wide sleeves, are of a piece with the body

Lathe-turned doll, made in 1983

Sides of bobbed hair are shaped as part of the head and defined with paint

The mark is screen-printed on the back of the head, over the painted hair.

Legs and arms have limited sideways and up-and-down movement

HAPPY DAYS GIRL (LEFT)
This 1930s English doll is made from flat pieces of wood, painted and varnished to show facial features, hair, and feet. The simple fixings at the shoulders and hips hold the arms and legs in place, and provide an effective, if basic, jointing system. Ht: 8in (20cm)

1920s FLAPPER (BELOW) This wooden spoon shows how household equipment can be transformed with a little imagination. Painted in black on white, with touches of red and gold, it is a stylish impression of a flapper. Ht: 12in (30cm)

Original poupard design, reinterpreted by a modern maker

1991 POUPARD (ABOVE) This fine piece of wood-turning is the work of doll artist Elizabeth Pongratz. Ht: 5½in (14cm)

BAVARIAN BABY (LEFT) A small doll has been decorated with oil-based paints. Ht: 3½in (9cm)

Dress, made of black nylon upholstery fringe, "dances" when spoon handle is twirled

CLOTHESPIN DOLL (RIGHT)
Straight, old-fashioned clothespins were often transformed by mothers into improvised playthings. The raffia hair of this c.1955 doll is ingeniously bound to fall on either side of its neck, so that the plaits form the doll's arms. Ht: 4½in (11.5cm)

Mouth and eyes are drawn with ballpoint pen

Metal rivets join limbs to torso

Clothes are made from rag-bag scraps of cotton material

Wood has been neither painted nor varnished

Penciled eyes, nostrils, and mouth

Carved nose

Slots in body sides allow arms to be raised and lowered

Convex sides of spoons form feet

TOMMY SPOONER (ABOVE) This character, made in the United States c.1896, is constructed from five wooden spoons attached to a carved, hollowed-out body. The legend on its back — "Pack carefully, do not handle" — may have been added at a later date. Ht: 12in (30cm)

Peg Woodens

· 1790s to the present day ·

JOINTED WOODEN DOLLS made after 1790 are usually called Dutch dolls or peg woodens. The first term may be a corruption of *deutsch*, meaning German – indicating their country of origin – or a reference to the Dutch ports through which they were exported from Germany to England. The second term refers to the use of pegs in the jointing and the fact that the dolls resemble straight, old-fashioned clothespins. Regardless of terminology, these dolls are united in being relatively simple turned and carved figures, which were usually painted only on the parts that were unclothed. ‿ Although World War II created a hiatus in the large-scale production of peg woodens, a recent awakening of interest in the old techniques, together with improved machinery and paints, has given these inexpensive dolls a new lease on life today.

The printed label, sewn into the dress, indicates that this doll was made in 1963 as a favor to mark the annual Convention of the United Federation of Doll Clubs, held in the United States.

Head and torso are carved as one unit

High carved comb on top of head

Head and chest area are finished with flesh-toned paint

Painted hair and facial features

Joints are neater than those on similar 19th-century dolls

Simply carved hands have thumbs but no fingers

Torso is shaped into broad, flat hips and a narrow waist

Straight, unshaped thighs

Lower legs have rounded calves and trim ankles

Mortise and tenon joints attach limbs to torso and give movement to lower legs and arms

Dainty black slippers are painted onto the feet

Lower legs are painted to show white stockings

Doll wears a dress in the style of a young lady of the late 19th century

TUCKCOMB DOLL, "ANGELITA" *Hand-crafted in the United States by S. Smith, this fully jointed peg wooden is a modern version of an 1850s German doll. The high comb, often painted yellow, was a fashionable hair ornament of that period. It is carved as one with the head, and is a special feature of early 19th-century wooden dolls.*

HT: 6½in (16.5cm)

Ht: 17in (43cm)

Largest doll has ball joints at shoulders and hips

PEG WOODEN PARADE (LEFT)
This set was produced in the Grödener Tal region of Austria between 1925 and 1940. The largest figure has a relatively sophisticated jointing system, and even the tiniest of the nine has peg joints at the shoulders and hips.

PONYTAIL PEG DOLL (RIGHT)
The decorative tuckcomb, a feature of early 19th-century, Grödener Tal-made peg woodens, has been reinterpreted in this c.1960 version and updated as a carved ponytail. It was made by English collector Faith Eaton. Ht: 5in (13cm)

Facial features and hair are painted over base of flesh-colored oils

Ht: 12in (30cm)

All dolls have painted black hair, blue eyes, and red mouths

Clothing conceals torso, carved from same piece of wood as the head

Ht: 10in (25cm)

Noses of three largest dolls made of wooden wedge, slotted into the face

Mortise and tenon joints at hips, shoulders, elbows, and knees

Ht: 6¾in (17cm)

Noses of middle-sized dolls are painted; smaller dolls have no nose

Ht: 4¼in (11cm)

Ht. 3¼in (8cm)

Ht: 1¾in (4.5cm)

Ht: 1in (2.5cm)

Ht: ⅝in (1.5cm)

Lower legs are sticklike, but still have painted shoe detail

Feet are always painted to represent shoes

1820s PEG WOODEN (BELOW)
Peasants in the Grödener Tal carved dolls like this one during the harsh winter months, when they could not work in the forests. Though made in quantity, each doll has its own special features. Ht: 3½in (9cm)

DOLL DRESSED AS A NUN
(RIGHT) Many of these cheap dolls were clothed to represent figures from everyday life. In 1920s rural Austria, nuns were very much part of the Catholic communities. Ht: 6in (15cm)

Hand-painted facial features

Woolen wimple and habit

Fully jointed doll is encased in glass-fronted wooden frame

Rounded head, with an elongated neck

Glass rosary beads, with a metal crucifix

Original coarse cotton dress, shawl, and apron

Flat arms have simple peg joints at the elbows

DOLL MOUNTED AS AN ORNAMENTAL PIN (ABOVE)
This early 1960s miniature peg wooden was made by S. Smith in the United States. It has a carved comb on top of the head and a safety pin on the back of the frame. Ht: 1in (2.5cm)

Composition Dolls

The collective term "composition" is used to describe a variety of pulped wood- or paper-based mixtures from which doll heads and bodies are made. Originally introduced as a less expensive alternative to wood, composition also had the advantage of being a more malleable material. Toward the end of the eighteenth century, exciting experiments took place in the development of papier-mâché – the doll industry's most favored type of composition.

FROM THE START, manufacturers found that the papier-mâché mixture could be pressed into molds for shaping. The revolutionary idea – which sprang to life in the 1800s, and had far-reaching effects for doll-making – was to mold the mixture *under pressure*. Treated in this way, papier-mâché was found to be a strong, durable material that lent itself easily to mass production by machine. This versatility could now be exploited to fashion a wide range of products other than doll parts, including ornaments, boxes, and furniture. After molding, a glutinous wash called size was applied to the objects. This eliminated the need for the expensive gesso layer that was used with wood (see page 11) and prepared an even ground for paint.

Manufacturers took great pride in developing their own specially formulated papier-mâché mixtures and kept the recipes a closely guarded secret. A variety of bizarre ingredients might be added to the basic pulp – rags, bread, crushed eggshells, or ground-up animal bones or bone ash, for example – that increased the strength of the molded material while reducing its raw cost. As most recipes were not recorded or patented, the precise formula of the composition mixture used for a particular doll is invariably unknown and can only be determined by expensive chemical analysis.

Getting the Formula Right

Other types of composition, still based on wood or paper, were developed from the mid-nineteenth century. The increased use of additives such as glue, flour, boiled sawdust, plaster, and anything else that was affordable and available, did not always produce a result that was as indestructible as the manufacturers claimed. Composition containing edible ingredients attracted rodents and insects; other mixtures were affected by temperature and humidity, and would swell or shrink according to changes in the weather.

Papier-mâché was the unrivaled success of all the experimentation, and became the most widely used type of composition for doll heads and, somewhat later, bodies. Its first practical application was in the making of shoulder heads; papier-mâché socket heads followed later, introduced in the third quarter of the nineteenth century. But papier-mâché composition really came into its own with the development of

COTTAGE INDUSTRY *(LEFT)*
The processes required to finish machine-made composition heads and limbs were usually carried out as piecework by families in their own homes. In this engraving, the man is painting the heads, while the woman is dressing the completed doll.

1850s GIRL *(RIGHT) Most wax-over-composition dolls were made in Germany. This doll has a wax-over-papier-mâché shoulder head and lower limbs, with a stuffed cloth torso and upper limbs. With its auburn mohair wig, sleeping glass eyes, and period costume, this doll is a fine example of its type. Ht: 12in (30cm)*

doll bodies, in particular those with jointed limbs. Its strength, durability, and lightness, as well as suitability for molding, enabled manufacturers to make a range of different body types. Thin wooden slats provided additional strength for the parts that would receive the greatest degree of stress: at the joints, and as supports built into the torso itself.

After sizing, the whole surface was painted with water-based, flesh-colored tones and varnished. This thin finishing layer of clear varnish tended to discolor with age, giving many old composition dolls a faint yellowish cast. Attempts to wash off the varnish can damage the doll. The appearance of

the original color tones changes, and the surface is left exposed and vulnerable to damage.

From the turn of the twentieth century onward, the material that had started out as a cheap substitute for wood and then bisque increased in popularity with manufacturers in both France and Germany. And in the United States – a country that had no tradition of making bisque dolls – composition was used for almost all dolls until it was superseded by modern plastics, such as polyethylene and vinyl, in the 1940s.

Wax-over-composition

The process of coating composition heads with a layer of wax to enhance the appearance of the doll heads evolved almost as soon as manufacturers realized the potential of machine-molding papier-mâché mixtures. This technique was used with other types of composition, along with other materials, but was found to be most successful when applied to papier-mâché composition. Unfortunately, one principal disadvantage of wax-over-composition was soon revealed: an unsightly deterioration in the smooth surface of the wax. Caused by the different rates at which the two layers of composition and wax expanded and contracted, this produced faults ranging from fine-line crazing to wide cracks. Manufacturers were never able to solve this problem. As a result, the production of wax-over composition doll parts came to an end during the first decade of the twentieth century.

BABY-WALKER DOLL *(LEFT) The all-composition construction of this c.1860s German doll extends even to its dress. The shoulder head is coated with a layer of wax. The doll's semi-mechanical movement allows its legs to move back and forth as the baby walker is wheeled along. Ht: 6in (15cm)*

KÄTHE KRUSE GIRL AND BOY *(RIGHT) These 1930s figures were designed by Käthe Kruse, a famous German maker who is usually associated with pressed felt dolls. Their composition socket heads were probably based on designs for cloth heads, made at an earlier period. Ht: 19in (48cm)*

Greiner and German Dolls

· 1840s to 1900s ·

ONE OF THE FOREMOST manufacturers of composition doll heads in the United States was Ludwig Greiner, based in Philadelphia. It was run by Greiner himself from 1840 to 1874. Thereafter, the company operated as Greiner Bros., in care of his sons, until 1883. Greiner was granted his first patent for a reinforced papier-mâché shoulder head in 1858. The patented recipe consisted of one pound each of pulped white paper, dry Spanish whiting, and rye flour; one ounce glue; and linen, which reinforced the heads. These were formed by pouring the mixture into plaster molds, and were then painted and varnished.

The large size of the heads dictated the use of correspondingly large bodies: most dolls with Greiner heads are over 13 inches in height. The stuffed bodies were either handmade by individuals, or were produced commercially by another company.

GREINER'S IMPROVED PATENT HEADS.
Pat. March 30th '58

Early Greiner dolls bear a label on the back of the shoulder plate, marked "PATENT HEADS." Later models include the patent extension date, 1872.

Molded wavy hair has corkscrew curls at the back of the head and center parting

Head and shoulder plate cast as one unit and painted

Molded and painted facial features

Well-defined closed mouth

Shoulder plate is glued onto the top of the torso

Stuffed cloth upper arms, torso, and legs

Kid lower arms

Hands have separate, stitched fingers and thumbs

Seam at hipline allows doll to sit

"Seam" lines at knees formed by age and handling

Cotton lawn dress covers four layers of petticoats and pantaloons with eyelet lace trim

Damage to shoe reveals toes, formed by stitching

GREINER PATENT HEAD *This naked lady clearly demonstrates a convention that applies to most dolls: the head is disproportionately large for the size of the body parts. The reason for this is that the head is intended to embody and convey the doll's individual "personality."*

HT: 24in (60cm)

Open mouth shows bamboo teeth

FINE MASS-PRODUCED DOLL
(LEFT) Sonneberg, in Germany, produced many composition dolls for export. This 19th-century model has a wig, added over the usual painted hair of the papier-mâché shoulder head, and a gusseted kid body: both are signs of a good-quality product. Ht: 20in (50cm)

THE LOWER END OF THE MARKET
(RIGHT) This papier-mâché shoulder head was also made in Sonneberg in the 1820s–1830s. The stuffed cloth torso lacks shape, while the legs end in stubby feet, without toes. The arms are unjointed and made of kid. Ht: 26in (65cm)

Painted hair, with brushstroke "curls"; no wig

Gracefully modeled kid hands

Toes are stitched, but not separate

Kid arms are stitched to resemble gloves

Simply styled hair is molded and painted

Painted facial features

Papier-mâché shoulder head; molded and painted hair

1840S PRE-GREINER DOLL
(BELOW) This doll closely resembles a Greiner, and it also has its origins in the United States. The papier-mâché shoulder head has molded and painted hair, which suggests a small boy's style; however, it could also serve as a girl's head. Ht: 40in (102cm)

Papier-mâché shoulder head, glued onto torso

Painted hazel eyes, with black pupils

Upper limbs and torso are tightly stuffed with sawdust

Closed mouth, painted red

Inset brown glass eyes; no pupils

Carved wooden lower arms and legs

Holes for sewing head onto cloth body

Open/closed mouth with molded teeth

HOLZ-MASSE HEAD
(ABOVE) The German firm Cuno and Otto Dressel registered "Holz-Masse," meaning wood pulp, as a trademark in 1875. The mark was applied to heads of papier-mâché, composition, or wax-over-composition. This shoulder head, made c.1890, is stamped with the symbol of a helmet with wings, which appeared as part of the original trademark. Ht: 6in (15cm)

Blue paper bands conceal joins; bands can also be red or green

LADY WITH PAINTED ORANGE SLIPPERS
(LEFT) Made in the 1830s, this doll is a typical Sonneberg export. The bands of blue paper at the elbows and knees cover and neaten the joins between the stuffed kid of the upper arms and legs and the carved wood of the lower limbs. Ht: 10in (25cm)

Real baby shoes, made of leather, date from 1869

Developments in Composition

· 1850s to 1930s ·

WHILE LENDING ITSELF ADMIRABLY to the construction of heads and large jointed bodies, composition proved to have two features that made it an unsatisfactory material for entire dolls: it was easily damaged, and its surface texture was subject to crazing, giving the dolls a worn appearance after only a short time. Yet some of the manufacturers found that composition had its advantages. Like bisque, it could be molded and painted – but unlike bisque, it did not need to be fired. After 1900, many companies were established, predominantly in Germany and the United States, manufacturing a wide range of inexpensive all-composition dolls, as well as those with stuffed cloth or kid bodies. One such company was Stephan Schilling, which operated in the town of Sonneberg, in Germany, from 1878 to 1928.

Blond mohair wig, pinned in curls

Sleeping glass eyes, with heavily painted lashes and brows

Stuffed cloth upper arms

Composition lower arms

Back of the right thigh is stamped with Schilling's winged angel head trademark, registered in 1895

Well-shaped composition lower legs

Closed, painted mouth

Composition shoulder head, glued onto torso

Spread-fingered hands; fingers and nails defined with red-painted lines

Stuffed cloth upper legs

Toes are molded, but not separate

Two lace-trimmed "tails," called lappets, at back of cap

Starched white cotton oversleeves

Scissors and bone-handled penknife on silver-plated chatelaine

Original period costume

Dress conceals undergarments, including green-and-white striped corset with elastic garters and black stockings

c.1900 SCHILLING DOLL *The English nanny who gave this doll to her charge in 1904 dressed it in an exact replica of her own uniform. Although it is of good quality for its type, the relative cheapness of the doll is indicated by the body, which is straw-filled; more expensive dolls were stuffed with animal hair or other soft fibers.*

HT: 24in (60cm)

Tufts of woolen hair
and earrings suggest
"ethnic" appearance

Accessories include a stork-
shaped hanger, swan's-
down powder puff, a
bristle brush, mirror,
and combs

Composition
socket head

Composition
bent arms

DOLL IN CANE BASKET

(RIGHT) This 1930s German
doll has a composition flange
neck head, an open mouth
showing two bottom teeth, and
sleeping glass eyes with metal
eyelids. Its stuffed stockinette torso
and limbs are stitch-jointed at the
shoulders and hips. Ht: 12in (30cm)

Composition
bent legs

"TOPSY" (ABOVE) Black dolls
representing babies and toddlers grew
in popularity during the 1920s and
1930s. As this c.1935 American
example shows, the heads were often
cast from the same molds as those used
for Caucasian dolls. Ht: 12in (30cm)

Ribbed silk skullcap,
with yellow silk braid-
and-tassel trim

Reverse
socket head

Inset glass
eyes; no pupils

"SUSAN" (BELOW) Versatile composition
could be tinted to produce a range of colors:
dolls designed to represent ethnic children
usually had hair painted black and skin
painted brown. No attempt has been made to
modify this doll's Caucasian features.
Ht: 18in (46cm)

Shiny light
brown glaze
indicates that
this is a good-
quality doll

C.1855 TODDLER DOLL (RIGHT)
Made in Sonneberg, Germany, this
black doll has realistic, molded, non-
Caucasian features. A bellows squeaker
is housed within the torso of its fully
jointed, papier-mâché, Mottschmann-
type body. Ht: 8in (20cm)

All-composition
construction,
jointed at
shoulders and
hips, with bent
limbs

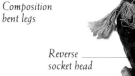

The mark on the back
of the neck clearly
identifies this model.

Gown conceals
stuffed cloth torso

Composition head,
with sleeping,
flirty glass eyes

Lower legs are
jointed at ankles

Unjointed bent
limbs made of
composition

SINGER SEWING MACHINE DOLL
(LEFT) This doll and its clothing, which
shows examples of machine stitching,
were used as a window display in one
of Singer's London stores during
World War II. It was made in the
late 1930s by Seyfarth and Reinhardt
of Germany, which operated from 1922
into the 1930s. Ht: 18in (46cm)

Original
organdy dress

Long gown, coat,
and bonnet are
decorated with
machine-quilting

Alexander Doll Company

· 1926 to the present day ·

IN 1926, SISTERS ROSE AND BERTHA ALEXANDER (who later changed her name to Beatrice) founded the Alexander Doll Company of New York. This firm is known even today for its quality products. Many of its early dolls were inspired by living or fictional characters, such as Shirley Temple or the glamorous heroine of *Gone With The Wind*, Scarlett O'Hara. On May 28, 1934, five little girls were born to the Dionne family just outside Montreal, in Canada. These babies quickly became media personalities, and many doll manufacturers grasped the marketing opportunity presented by such a novel event. However, only the Alexander Doll Co. was granted the right to register the Dionne Quintuplets as a trademark in 1936 in the United States. This set of dolls formed part of the firm's highly collectible Madame Alexander line.

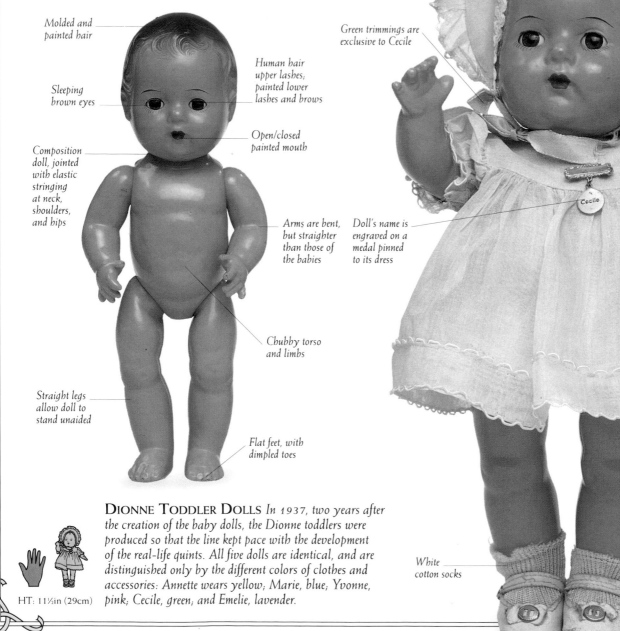

Molded and painted hair

Sleeping brown eyes

Composition doll, jointed with elastic stringing at neck, shoulders, and hips

Straight legs allow doll to stand unaided

Human hair upper lashes; painted lower lashes and brows

Open/closed painted mouth

Arms are bent, but straighter than those of the babies

Chubby torso and limbs

Flat feet, with dimpled toes

Green trimmings are exclusive to Cecile

Doll's name is engraved on a medal pinned to its dress

White cotton socks

Cloth ankle-strap shoes, with metal buckles on toes and snap fastenings

DIONNE TODDLER DOLLS *In 1937, two years after the creation of the baby dolls, the Dionne toddlers were produced so that the line kept pace with the development of the real-life quints. All five dolls are identical, and are distinguished only by the different colors of clothes and accessories: Annette wears yellow; Marie, blue; Yvonne, pink; Cecile, green; and Emelie, lavender.*

HT: 11½in (29cm)

PHYSICIAN AND NURSE (*LEFT*) Dr. Allan Roy Dafoe and the nurse, Louise De Kirilene, who had attended the birth of the Dionne babies, were also part of the Dionne Quintuplets set. Made of composition, the dolls are jointed at the shoulders and hips, and have mohair wigs. The physician's features are all painted; the nurse has sleeping brown eyes. Ht: Physician 13½in (34cm); Nurse 13in (33cm)

Wrist tag is identical to that of the physician; the reverse side is shown

Original wrist tag of the Alexander Doll Co.

BABY DOLLS (*BELOW*) The first generation of Madame Alexander Dionne Quintuplet babies were issued in Spring 1935. Their bent legs allow the dolls to sit but not stand, unlike the toddlers, which stand unaided. Ht: 7in (18cm)

DOLL MARKS

Most dolls have the name "ALEXANDER" molded on the back of the neck or back of the torso. Other variations include "Mme. Alexander" or "ALEX."

The reverse of this gold wrist tag reads "AN / ALEXANDER / PRODUCT / SUPREME / QUALITY / AND / DESIGN."

Created by **MADAME ALEXANDER** *New York*

CECILE *in green*

EMELIE *in lavender*

ANNETTE *in yellow*

MARIE *in blue*

YVONNE *in pink*

Each painted wooden crib is equipped with a pink mattress, a pillow with ruffled case, and a Swiss cotton ribbon-trimmed quilt

Original wrist tag reads "All Rights Reserved Throughout the World on Dolls/ ALEXANDER DOLL CO. • NEW YORK"

Wooden cribs are 4½in (11.5cm) wide, 9in (23cm) long, and 5½in (14cm) high

Wax-over-composition Dolls

· 1830s to 1900s ·

THE IDEA OF ENHANCING composition with wax was realized by many German doll-head makers starting in c.1830. Between 1870 and 1900, a small number of English companies in London also manufactured wax-over-composition heads; these were attached to stuffed cloth bodies. The English dolls are usually very well marked with body stamps; if there are no markings, wax-over-composition dolls are usually assumed to be of German origin.

 The manufacturing process involved applying a thin layer of wax over heads, and also limbs, made of composition, to give the surface a smoother and more natural appearance. Wax-over-composition dolls looked better than those made of composition alone; they also had the advantage of being significantly cheaper – both to manufacture and to buy – than their poured wax relatives (see pages 30–41).

Silk-lined velvet hat is tied with lace-trimmed organdy ribbons and secured with blue glass-headed hatpins

Curled auburn mohair wig

Molded and painted mouth shows two rows of small teeth

Inset blue-gray glass eyes

Cape is made of silk and poplin

Finely modeled shoulder head has a thin tinted layer of wax over its composition base

Wax-over-composition arms

Starched cotton apron over a button-fronted cotton bodice and skirt

Glazed cotton upper legs and torso are stuffed with straw

Composition lower legs

Feet are molded and painted to show stylish side-buttoning boots with heels

C.1900 GERMAN DOLL

The young owner who dubbed this pretty lady "Nurse Cross" could hardly have chosen a less apt name, for the doll's half-smiling expression radiates anything but displeasure. The costume is a detailed replica of the uniform worn by a child's nanny in England c.1900.

HT: 17in (43cm)

Penny toy bought from street vendor on Ludgate Hill, London

Shoulder head is made of plaster

C.1830 BAGMAN'S BABY (LEFT)

Cheap German-made dolls were once a common item of merchandise for peddlers, often referred to in England at the time as "Bagmen." The method of inserting the wig into the head through a vertical groove cut in the crown also gives these dolls the name of "slit-head." Ht: 27in (68cm)

Pink kid arms; separate fingers and thumbs

Dress conceals stuffed cloth torso and legs

Costume conceals hard, stuffed cloth upper legs and torso, stitched at hips

Beneath dress, a wire protruding through the base of the lower torso opens and closes the glass eyes

Elaborate, felt-topped head-dress, made of black animal fur and secured with a "gold" chain chinstrap

Auburn mohair wig

Open mouth shows three teeth

Sleeves hide unjointed composition arms

Hands have separate thumbs and joined fingers, delineated with painted red lines

SCOTTISH COSTUME DOLL (LEFT)

Typical of dolls produced in Germany and exported throughout Europe, this finely dressed 1890s model has a wax-over-composition shoulder head, and unjointed arms and lower legs of composition. The inset blue glass eyes have light irises and darker pupils, and are an advance on the pupilless eyes of many earlier models. Ht: 14in (35cm)

Handmade Highland Regimental costume

C.1860 GERMAN DOLL WITH ALICE BAND (RIGHT)

Fashionable hairstyles, sometimes accessorized, as shown in this example, were molded with the head and painted before the application of the wax coating. Dolls with molded and painted hair tended to be less expensive than those with either human hair or mohair wigs. Ht: 18in (46cm)

Lead-weighted sleeping eyes, with metal eyelids

Dress conceals body, made in the 1850s, which predates the doll's c.1860s head

Wooden lower arms with spoon-shaped hands

Wooden lower legs, painted to show flat-heeled boots

LATE 19TH-CENTURY GIRL (RIGHT)

Thick wax covers the composition of this German shoulder head, and a lead-weight mechanism operates the sleeping glass eyes. The hands are well modeled, yet the maker has not cleaned up the casting lines at the ends of the fingers. Ht: 17½in (45cm)

Ash blond mohair wig

Printed cotton dress is older than the doll

Composition lower arms and legs

Poured Wax Dolls

One of the original uses for wax was for making religious effigies and votive offerings. This practice, widespread in Roman Catholic parts of Europe, gave many makers their first experience in wax modeling. Seeking new expression for their creativity, these craftsmen carried their skills to London, where, by the nineteenth century, they had established an unrivaled tradition of wax doll-making.

SOME OF THE MOST inspired European doll-makers worked in England between 1850 and 1930. Their originality was matched by their choice of material: translucent, luminous, and warm to the touch, wax is perfectly suited to creating dolls, in particular portrait dolls, which rely on the faithful reproduction of facial features and skin tones for their realism.

Casting the Head

The nineteenth-century wax modelers all followed the same technical, yet simple, process to create their doll heads. The first stage involved the skilled modeling of the head in wax or clay. From this, a cast was produced in the form of a two- or three-part plaster mold. The molten wax mixture, a blend of coloring, bleached beeswax, and a number of other additives, was poured into the mold. It was allowed only a brief time to set

before the excess mixture was poured out. Some heads were made with a single pouring; others were built up using multiple layers of wax, a method which produced a stronger head with a more translucent, skinlike texture. In either case, the final thickness of the wax was no more than ⅛in (3mm). After the wax had cooled and solidified, the casting was lifted from the mold, and any traces of the casting lines were removed from the sides of the head.

It was the finishing processes that determined whether or not the head was a good one. Blown or molded glass eyes, set into the cut-out and shaped eye sockets, were fixed with either a small extra amount of wax, or warming the socket to melt the surrounding wax. Sleeping eyes are rarely found in poured wax heads, but when used were normally on a push–pull wire. The standard type of lead-weight mechanism can cause damage inside the head if it knocks about. The doll's hair was applied next,

1806 ENGLISH DOLL *(LEFT) This small, beady-eyed figure shows the special feature of early dolls: a shoulder head and lower limbs molded entirely from solid wax. Its feet have been cast and dipped in green-colored wax to resemble shoes. The torso and upper limbs are made of stuffed cloth. Ht: 6in (13cm)*

PLASTER MOLD *(RIGHT) Cast wax doll heads are always hollow, and made in a mold of three or, as seen here, two parts. The two lugs at the top fit snugly into correspondingly positioned holes on the other half of the mold, which forms the back of the head.*

Montanari
180
Soho Bazaar.

THE MANUFACTURE OF GERMAN WAX DOLLS (LEFT)

This engraving, reproduced in the November 26, 1887, edition of The Queen, The Lady's Newspaper, *illustrates the following eight steps, showing how a wax-headed doll was created and finished: 1. Making the Model; 2. Joining the Head; 3. Setting the Eyes; 4. Waxing the Head; 5. Painting the Face; 6. Dressing the Hair; 7. Fixing the Head; 8. Dressing the Finished Doll.*

MONTANARI MARK (ABOVE)

Wax heads are rarely signed, but their cloth bodies may carry the maker's name. Mme. Montanari's handwritten signatures sometimes include her business address, as here.

ensure an exact color match, heads and limbs for complete sets of dolls were produced during the same casting session. Most poured wax arms were cast to above the elbow joint, and legs to above the knee. These, too, had grommets embedded in the wax, and were attached to the upper stuffed cloth limbs the same way as the head was to the torso.

In what was still largely a home-based business, each one of these steps in the finishing process was assigned to a particular member of the family. Enduring very poor conditions, and dealing with dangerous materials, many of the workers paid a high price for their occupation. Molten wax, which was poured at extremely high temperatures, often caused severe burns; the materials with which the bodies were stuffed contained tiny particles of dust that, if inhaled, could lead to breathing difficulties; but perhaps the most hazardous of all was the white lead used to color the wax, which proved to be an insidious – and in some instances deadly – poison.

inserted as either single strands or as small clumps into fine cuts or pinholes in the head. (Hair eyelashes were similarly inset.) This way, the hair seems to grow from the scalp; it has more natural movement than can be achieved with a wig; and it enhances the realistic appearance of the head itself. Both human hair and mohair were used; sometimes the two were combined on the same head. Buyers could even have snippings of their own child's hair inset at almost no additional cost. Finally, coloring was applied to the mouth and the whole surface was dusted with fine pumice to remove the shine.

Completing the Doll

Poured wax heads usually have deep shoulder plates. The head is sewn to the body through a hole at each of the lower corners of the front and back plates. In better quality dolls, grommets or metal eyelets reinforce the holes and protect them from wear and tear. The cloth bodies, usually rather lumpy in shape, are made of calico. They are stuffed with cow or other animal hair, or woolly fibers, but rarely sawdust. To

1980S PORTRAIT DOLL

(RIGHT) This is doll number 4001 in a limited-edition series of 5,000 portrait dolls that represent Peggy Nisbet. The dolls were designed by the House of Nisbet in consultation with Faith Eaton – an English doll authority – to commemorate the company's founder. Ht: 18in (46cm)

Early Dolls

· 1750s to 1850s ·

THE MAJORITY OF WAX-HEADED DOLLS that have survived date from the past two centuries. Even the earliest of these dolls show the skill of the wax modeler. Most were expensive to buy, so it is quite unlikely that they were ever treated as throw-away items. The fact that only a few were made is a more satisfactory explanation for their relative scarcity now, than questions of quality.

Many wax dolls appear to be almost exact copies of each other. However, their similarity merely reflects contemporary fashion and style, as with modern-day favorites like Barbie or G.I. Joe. For example, wax doll heads created between 1750 and 1850 are modeled to show a high forehead. In Georgian England, this was a visible sign of good breeding and refined sensibility.

Inset glass eyes, another common feature, are pupilless and black in pre-1820s dolls. By the 1830s, makers could choose colored eyes, which were usually blue glass with black pupils, to give their dolls a more realistic expression.

Wax shoulder head, with inset pupilless black glass eyes

Molded and painted facial features

Satin stole is a later addition

Painted brownish black curly hair shows a typical style of the period

Sleeves conceal stuffed-cloth upper arms

Lower arms to above elbow joint are made of wax

Ears are simple shapes, set close to the sides of the head

Dress conceals stuffed upper legs and torso, made of striped mattress ticking

Shoulder plate is very deep

Off-white, very fine cotton muslin dress, with petticoat and bloomers beneath

1812 HEIRLOOM DOLL, "BESSIE"

The essence of any doll is conveyed in its head, and this fine example of early wax modeling suggests an accomplished maker. Lovely "Bessie" was the homecoming gift of Captain Nathaniel Osgood – a young shipmaster living in the Atlantic seaboard town of Salem, Massachusetts – to his small daughter, Elizabeth.

HT: 20in (50cm)

Inset auburn
human hair

Wax head to
base of neck;
upper torso made
of calico painted
in flesh tones

Upper arms, torso,
and legs are made
of stuffed calico

Wax lower
arms

Beneath the dress, doll
wears a complete set of
linen undergarments

Wooden cradle decorated
with Regency-patterned
paper and bead finials

Inset mohair and
painted facial features
on all three dolls

Red-painted
shoes are hollow
and very fragile

SHADOWBOX TRIO (ABOVE) All-
wax, hollow dolls are usually quite
small, because of their fragility. Made
in England and Germany from 1790
to 1820, they were popular ornaments,
and were often displayed in a glass-
fronted case. Ht: 1½–2½in (4–6cm)

Pale wax
shoulder head

Dress conceals stuffed
calico upper arms,
torso, and legs

1758 COSTUME DOLL (ABOVE)
Young English lady Laetitia Clark
designed and made this splendid silk
outfit, which she called "A Long Robe
Coat Dress for a Lady of Sixteen." The
doll itself is nicely modeled, but owes its
fame entirely to its clothes and their
maker. Ht: 13in (33cm)

Wax
shoulder
head

Poured wax lower
arms to above
elbow joint

Dress conceals stuffed
cloth legs and torso
stitched at hips

Inset bright blue
glass eyes, with
pupils

Red molded
wax shoes

1757 "PARTY DRESS" DOLL
(ABOVE) This simple costume was
also designed and sewn by Laetitia
Clark (see top left). Red was widely
used for doll footwear at this period.
By the end of the 1790s, green was
the favored color. Ht: 8in (20cm)

TWIN SISTERS (LEFT) Made in
England c.1838 and representing
twins, these dolls are identical –
something of a rarity – down to
their lace-trimmed pantalettes. The
fading of the shoulder heads to pale
beige is due to natural changes in
the wax. Ht: 20in (50cm)

Hand-stitched
leather shoes

Original, fine
cotton clothing

English Makers

· 1850s to 1930s ·

TOWARD THE MIDDLE of the nineteenth century, wax became an increasingly popular material for creating doll heads and limbs. By far the greatest exponents of the craft were the English-born and émigré, often Italian, makers who were based in London. During the next 50 years, wax doll-making reached its zenith, particularly with the achievements of such virtuosi as the Pierottis (see pages 36–39) and Montanaris. Examples of their work were displayed and won prizes at international exhibitions.

⟋ The Great Exhibition of 1851, held at the Crystal Palace in London's Hyde Park, helped to establish the reputations of many makers. Madame Augusta Montanari won her first medal at this event. A great number of her dolls were portraits, some of which represented Queen Victoria's children. Perhaps it was this, rather than the medal she won, that earned her the patronage of the queen.

Blue glass eyes, set into sockets

Two grommets, for sewing head to torso

Poured wax lower arms, cast to include the elbow joints

Chubby baby hands and wrists

Legs can bend at seamed knees

Hip seams attach legs to stuffed calico torso and allow doll to sit

Poured wax lower legs; feet have well-defined toes showing toenails

Quilted and ruched silk bonnet, tied with satin ribbons

Blond hair is set into the head in small clumps

Three-tiered carrying cape

Lavish silk tassel and braid trimming

HT: 26in (65cm)

MONTANARI DOLL
A usual practice among makers of this time was to team baby heads and limbs with adult bodies. True baby-doll bodies had shapeless torsos, but because the body was intended to be covered up, its form scarcely mattered. This 1870s Montanari baby doll is dressed in period Edwardian clothing.

Long lawn robe was everyday late 19th-century baby attire

Inset human hair

Wax shoulder head, colored in pink tones

Sleeves cover stuffed calico upper arms

Very full head of inset human hair

Inset auburn human hair

Wax shoulder head; modeled facial features represent those of a young girl

Meech's southeast London workshop address is stamped on the doll's thigh.

Wire-operated, sleeping brown glass eyes

Wood-handled silk parasol opens and closes

Lower arms to above elbow are made of wax

LUCY PECK HEAD (ABOVE)
A high proportion of beeswax used in the casting gives this c.1900 shoulder head its dark flesh tone. Ht: 27in (68cm)

BY ROYAL APPOINTMENT
(ABOVE) This 1883 shoulder head shows the talent of Londoner Herbert John Meech, who worked between 1865 and 1917. Royal patronage entitled him to use the crest that he included with many of his body stamps. Ht: 23in (58cm)

"C. C." incised on the sole is the mark of an unidentified maker

Dress conceals stuffed calico upper legs and torso

Pale wax lower legs and arms

LUCY PECK GIRL (ABOVE) From
1891 to 1930, Lucy Peck made dolls and ran a repair service. She designed and created this 1890s example, but the dolls she repaired would often also bear her firm's mark. Ht: 20in (50cm)

The ink stamp appears on the back of the doll's torso.

1880s SOHO BAZAAR DOLL
(RIGHT) Charles Marsh came from a famous family of doll-makers and repairers, and worked between 1878 and 1895. His dolls are wax-over-composition, wax-over-papier-mâché, or poured wax, as here. Ht: 18in (46cm)

Human hair from the future owner was often inset into the doll's head

Inset glass eyes; human hair lashes and brows

The stamp on the doll's torso clearly identifies the maker.

The Pierotti Family

· 1770s to 1935 ·

THE PIEROTTIS WERE NOT SIMPLY doll-makers. They were (and called themselves) wax modelers. The company was established by Domenico Pierotti, an Italian who married an English girl and learned the essential skills of plaster mold-making as well as wax casting and modeling from her family. One of their 12 children, Anerico Cephas, born 1809, carried the wax-modeling business forward and perfected the poured wax method for the production of heads. His son, Charles William, was also an innovative wax modeler. Many of the designs created by these two were adapted by later members of the family. In 1935, with the retirement of Charles Ernest, Charles William's son, four generations of family business came to an end.

Straw boater is contemporary, but not original to doll

Inset violet-blue glass eyes

Long titian mohair inserted into the wax

Eyebrows and lashes of mohair match that of hair

Clothing belonged to a real child and dates from 1872

Stuffed cloth upper arms are sewn to torso under the shoulder plate

Threads, waxed with resin, attach the shoulder head to the torso

Upper legs, made separately from the torso, attached with seams at hips

Calico torso, stuffed with cowhair

Lower limbs are secured to upper limbs by thread through the grommets

Hands have dimpled knuckles and short, stubby fingers

Lower legs have shaped calves, and feet showing insteps

Hem of dress is decorated with pattern of trailing vine leaves

Socks and shoes are made of silk

HT: 24in (60cm)

HENRY PIEROTTI, GIRL *Anerico Cephas Pierotti is usually known by the anglicized name Henry. This doll, which he made c.1870, represents a young girl. Its wax shoulder head and lower limbs are colored peach, rather than the standard pink. The doll's straw boater, cotton dress, and silk socks and shoes belonged to a child, and date from 1872.*

1920s FORTUNE TELLER

(LEFT) Charles Ernest Pierotti made this unique doll to raise money at a Masonic bazaar. It has a legless body fitted onto a wooden stick handle. As the stick was twirled, streamers with fortunes flew out, like the ribbons of a maypole. The shoulder head and limbs are made of darkly colored wax, which gives the doll an exotic and gypsylike appeararance.
Ht: 27in (68cm)

Inset brown glass eyes

Black hair is a combination of inset human hair and mohair

Costume, made by Eleanor Bessie Pierotti, cannot be removed

Hands have slender, delicate fingers and thumbs

Gracefully modeled wax lower arms

Skirt would have had cloth and paper streamers attached to the waistband

Wooden stick is joined to doll's stuffed cloth torso

Head made of thin, single layer of wax

Portrait head of an unknown old man

Portrait head of young woman; finished portrait heads were discarded if not true likenesses

Blown glass eyes are rounded and bulbous

Blue, gray, or brown eyes were used for portrait dolls, depending on color of person's eyes

Molded glass eyes are lozenge-shaped

Wooden sticks, joined with strips of linen gauze

Crown is set with "pearls" and encrusted with colored glass "gems"

Inset blue glass eyes, with pupils

Blue velvet Cap of Estate, inside the crown, is edged with miniver

Inset human hair, braided and coiled around head

Pale wax shoulder head

Fur tippet is draped over top of cloak

Darker wax arms, cast to above elbow joint

Fur-trimmed velvet cloak covers the naked back of the doll

Crown shows "scar" where head was cut to insert eyes and then repaired

Silk and net, sequined gown extends only to doll's sides

Titian mohair, wound around sticks, is curled into ringlets

C.1840 QUEEN VICTORIA

(ABOVE) Henry Pierotti was an especially gifted wax modeler, and created many of the portrait dolls for which the family became famous. The strong resemblance of this model to the young queen is a testament to his ability. Ht: 19in (48cm)

PROTOTYPES AND PARTS

(LEFT) Experiments formed a vital element of the Pierottis' work, and not all resulted in viable products. Prototype heads, like these of an old man and a young woman, were made of a single layer of very thin and fragile wax. The eyes and hair were particularly important features, helping to give the dolls expression and personality.

Pierotti Portrait Dolls

· 1900s to 1930s ·

WAX MODELERS were quick to discover that the material offered unique possibilities for rendering highly realistic portrait heads. Members of royal families, soldiers, and statesmen were all popular subjects. Henry Pierotti was one of a few wax portrait modelers who created dolls representing Queen Victoria (see page 37) and Lord Roberts (see below). Other dolls have no known sitter, but are clearly portraits – perhaps of friends or family – to judge by their idiosyncratic facial features and expressions.
Carrying the realism further, the Pierottis introduced three styles of body that corresponded to the age and gender of the person the doll was to represent. The standard shape – chubby shoulders, a narrow waist, and broad hips – was used for most of the dolls, except those portraying babies and men.

White mohair, inset to show a receding hairline

Blown glass eyes with mohair brows and upper lashes

Mohair mustache and goatee

Brownish patina often forms as the wax ages

Long, stuffed cloth arms; typical feature of male dolls

Full dress uniform, decorated with gold braid, brass buttons, ceremonial medals, and rank insignia

Shoulder head is secured to torso by thread through grommets

Large poured wax hands, cast to above wrist joint; typical feature of male dolls

Hamley Bros. tag: the Regent Street, London, toyshop was formerly located at 812 Oxford Street

Lower half of stuffed cloth torso extends to form the upper legs; typical feature of male dolls

Sleeve slash and stripe denote rank of Commander-in-Chief

White kid breeches

Poured wax lower legs; only one style was made

Black leather gaiters and black leather shoes, made to represent boots

Sword, sheathed in a leather scabbard

HT: 20in (50cm)

LORD ROBERTS AND MALE DOLL BODY
This tribute to Lord Roberts – Commander-in-Chief of the British Army during the Boer War – was modeled by Charles Ernest Pierotti c. 1900, adapted from an earlier model created by Charles William Pierotti. The naked doll shows the characteristics of the male body style.

STANDARD BABY HEAD

(RIGHT) Pierotti nonportrait baby dolls have one style of head. The eyes are of inset blue glass, with blond mohair lashes and brows; the hair is also inset blond mohair. A delicate pursing of the lips gives the mouth a bowed, slightly open shape. Ht: 20in (50cm)

Mohair is set into the head in small clumps

Childlike nose, with broad bridge

Molded, closed mouth, painted red

Shoulder head has a short, thick neck and plump chest

C.1900 PORTRAIT BABY HEAD

(LEFT) Charles Ernest Pierotti produced this portrait of his only child, Patrick Enrico, who died when still very young. The fragile beauty of the infant is evident in the subtle pink coloring of the wax, the large pale blue glass eyes, and the gold-blond mohair curled over the forehead and around the sides of the face. Ht: 22in (55cm)

Lace-trimmed silk robe, adorned with cream satin ribbons and French knots

Inset mohair or human hair

Standard poured wax baby shoulder head

Blue eyes were usual; buyers could choose other colors

No grommets in sew holes on cheaper models

Inset blue glass eyes, with painted facial features

Well-defined chin and jawline

Inset long strawberry-blond mohair, caught up at back of head into a loose braid

Pale wax shoulder head has a slim neck

Elaborate leg-o'-mutton dress sleeves, with stitched knife-pleating

Fingerless lace mittens have half-thumbs

Joined fingers and separate thumbs

Small feet are in proportion to the hands

HEAD PROFILE

(ABOVE) The elegant curves of this young woman's head and shoulders contrast with the chubby, fleshy modeling of the neck and shoulders of the Pierotti baby dolls.

C.1905 BABY DOLL

(ABOVE) The stuffed calico or glazed cotton torso of the stylized baby body is waistless, and usually extends to the upper legs, unless the doll is large. The upper arms, of the same fabric, are sewn to the torso under the shoulder plate. The poured wax lower arms are cast to above the bent elbow joint. Ht: 12in (30cm)

COSTUME DISPLAY DOLL

(RIGHT) In the early 20th century, fashionable London shops and dress designers enticed would-be clients with miniature versions of their latest creations, exhibited on doll models. This c.1910 portrait of a young lady displays an off-the-shoulder striped silk taffeta evening gown. The fine shoulder head is teamed with the narrow-waisted, stuffed cloth body that was used for all dolls except babies and men. Ht: 16in (40cm)

"Princess Daisy"

· 1890s ·

SEEN IN THE LIGHT of their quirky history, some otherwise rather unremarkable dolls can acquire great charm. In 1894, when Miss Twiss, living in Amsterdam, Holland, purchased a rather plain English wax doll, the city was preparing to host the International Exposition that was to be held the following year. Miss Twiss had the idea of commissioning Dutch craftsmen to make clothes and accessories for the doll, which would be used as a model to display their work at the exposition.

The display was purchased by a group of English ladies, who presented the doll, "Princess Daisy," and her extensive trousseau to Princess Mary of Teck (who was later queen to George V, King of England) as a christening gift for her daughter Mary, born in 1897.

Inset very pale blond mohair

Poured wax shoulder head

Rosettes and streamers, attached to waist ribbon, match those on the bonnet

Sleeping blue glass eyes; mohair eyebrows and upper lashes

Wide band of cream moiré silk ribbon, tied in a bow, secures the doll to its cushion

Poured wax lower arms, cast to above elbow joint

Stuffed calico upper limbs and torso

Buttoned, padded drawers, worn over diapers

Darker bands of calico cover the joins

Poured wax lower legs, cast to above knee joint

Muslin christening robe, inset with broderie anglaise

HT: 18in (46cm)

CEREMONIAL PRESENTATION "Princess Daisy" is displayed lying on her own christening cushion, as was the custom in late 19th-century England when babies were presented for baptism. The cotton lawn cushion is padded with eiderdown and has a slipcover of silk-embroidered, lace-edged muslin. The doll wears a lace bonnet, trimmed with silk ribbon rosettes, and a traditional christening robe over a satin underdress and linen undergarments.

Handmade brass clothes stands are part of the doll's accessories

Decorative pink satin bows on shoulders of dress

Pink ribbon sash matches the satin bows on the shoulders

ROYAL APPAREL (LEFT) Miss Twiss provided an inventory, listing each piece of clothing in "Princess Daisy's" wardrobe. Every item uses only the finest natural materials — muslin, silk, satin, and wool — and is embroidered with either the initial "D" or the doll's name, "Daisy," depending on its size.

CANOPIED CRADLE (BELOW) The specially commissioned accessories include a wrought-iron stand with curlicued stretchers and legs, which allows the metal cradle to swing gently to and fro; six top and bottom sheets, pillowcases, and blankets; and an ivory cross with winged cherub, to ensure "Princess Daisy" sweet dreams.

Afternoon dress, made of cotton lawn and embroidered with daisies

Large satin bows and rosettes decorate almost every item

Satin traveling cloak, with lace-trimmed cape and elaborate lace collar

LAYETTE BASKET AND CHRISTENING GIFTS (BELOW) The satin-lined basket contains myriad accessories, including a real sponge in an oiled silk bag, tiny safety pins, soaps, and a silver bed-warmer. Only the rubber nipples for the baby bottles and the box of special cookies have perished with time.

Satin and lace bonnet hangs on its own brass hat stand

Two-layered canopy, made of Swiss dot cotton over satin

Padded satin quilt

Wooden sock hangers

Basket stands on four plaited wicker feet

Hallmarked silver spoons and fork

Real gold "Daisy" name pin and bracelet

Real pearl necklace, with a pavé diamond clasp

Forged iron cradle and stand, painted white, with gold paint edging and trim

Porcelain Dolls

One of the most fascinating aspects of language is that individual words — which have precise definitions — can take on a variety of imprecise connotations in everyday speech. The word "porcelain," for example, seems to acquire different meanings when used by different people. As a term in our special doll language, however, porcelain describes with a single word three types of doll head: glazed china; untinted bisque; and bisque.

THE PRODUCTION OF porcelain doll heads was rarely the principal output of any manufacturer, so it is useful to understand the development of porcelain as a doll-making material in its historical context. This very fine grade of ceramicware is fired in a kiln at not less than 2,372°F (1,300°C). Few clays are able to withstand such extreme temperatures: feldspathic china clay, or kaolin, and china stone are two that can.

The discovery of these clays in parts of Germany at the beginning of the eighteenth century led to the establishment of the Meissen factory, near Dresden, in 1709. In Cornwall, in southwestern England, clay-pits revealed sufficient reserves for the first manufacture of porcelain items in 1770. Extensive deposits of these naturally occurring clays were mined throughout Germany, especially in the region of Thuringia. The porcelain industry flourished there, with a number of factories churning out inexpensive figurines and decorative ornaments, as well as the exquisite domestic tableware that was their stock in trade. For many manufacturers, the production of doll heads was nothing more than a lucrative sideline.

Moldings and Castings

After the start of the nineteenth century, porcelain began to enjoy increasing favor with the doll-head manufacturers. This popularity lasted for the next hundred years or so, when porcelain was supplanted by the new, more versatile compositions and plastics introduced in the first quarter of the twentieth century. All the porcelain doll heads that were manufactured in

GLAZED CHINA DOLLS *(LEFT) In the United States, all three of these dolls are called Frozen Charlottes. In Britain, the larger figures are known as Bath Dolls. At Christmas, the smaller ones were often hidden inside plum puddings as good-luck charms, earning them the name Pudding Dolls. Ht: Largest 18in (46cm); smallest 1in (2.5cm)*

UNTINTED BISQUE SHOULDER HEAD *(RIGHT) Dolls made in the late 1860s classical style owe much to the ideas of ancient Greece and Rome. The typical formality of the style, shown in the modeling of this German doll's head, is echoed in the Greek key pattern that decorates its pretty cotton dress. Ht: 16in (40cm)*

the nineteenth century were produced in molds. Like those used in poured wax castings (see pages 30–31), these were made of plaster and in two or three parts. In the early days, a porcelain mixture with a malleable, doughlike consistency was pressed into the molds for shaping. Refining their production techniques, manufacturers introduced a wetter fluid mixture that could be poured rather than pressed into the molds.

Glazing and Finishing

The heads were usually given three separate firings and two layers of glaze. The initial firing produced biscuitware, or bisque, so called because of its close, brittle texture. The second and third firings fused the painted decorations and glazes. After the firings, the appearance of the heads identifies each of the three different types: glazed china heads are those with a shiny overglaze; untinted bisque heads have a matte finish and are usually white; bisque heads are tinted with a tinge of color. Manufacturers produced both shoulder and socket heads, and achieved equally good results with pressed and poured porcelain. From the outside, pressed heads cannot be distinguished from poured ones and give no clue to the casting method

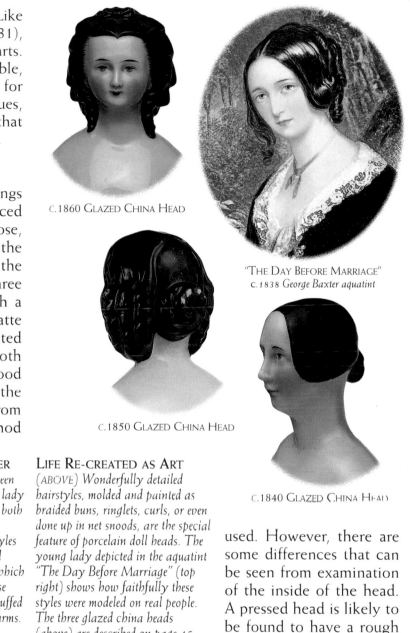

C.1860 GLAZED CHINA HEAD

"THE DAY BEFORE MARRIAGE"
c.1838 George Baxter aquatint

C.1850 GLAZED CHINA HEAD

C.1840 GLAZED CHINA HEAD

GLAZED CHINA SHOULDER HEAD (LEFT) *Similarities between this doll and the untinted bisque lady at far left are no coincidence, as both were made in Germany c.1865.*
Likenesses include the hairstyles and facial features; pierced ears; the shoulder plate, which displays a molded blouse with a bow; and the stuffed cloth body with kid arms.
Ht: 21in (53cm)

LIFE RE-CREATED AS ART (ABOVE) *Wonderfully detailed hairstyles, molded and painted as braided buns, ringlets, curls, or even done up in net snoods, are the special feature of porcelain doll heads. The young lady depicted in the aquatint "The Day Before Marriage" (top right) shows how faithfully these styles were modeled on real people. The three glazed china heads (above) are described on page 45.*

used. However, there are some differences that can be seen from examination of the inside of the head. A pressed head is likely to be found to have a rough inner surface and will be uneven in thickness; the insides of poured heads, on the other hand, are smooth and consistently even.

∽ The fine texture of porcelain allowed the delicate molding of much ornamental detail. Many porcelain doll heads were cast to show the fashionable hairstyles of the period, and these usually also have molded and painted eyes. Other heads were left plain: the crown was cut away so that glass eyes could be inserted, and a wig was attached as part of the finishing process.

∽ Molded hairstyles were largely replaced by hair wigs after 1870, as they were considered to be more natural. The introduction of porcelain character dolls in the early twentieth century saw a revival in molded and painted hair, but the extremely decorative styles of the mid-nineteenth century were never repeated.

Fancy Glazed China Heads

· 1830s to 1880s ·

WHEN GERMAN MAKERS introduced the first porcelain doll heads with molded hairstyles in the 1830s, a variety of quality dolls came onto the market. These early shoulder heads are called glazed chinas because they are overglazed – a finish that makes them glossy while retaining the whiteness of the porcelain. The coloring of the cheeks and facial features is fixed in the underglaze, but it is quite rare for such heads to be tinted overall with flesh tones.

Reflecting real-life trends, the styling and adornment of the dolls' hair closely followed contemporary fashions. The clothing that was designed for the finished glazed china dolls was equally modish, and usually shows the most up-to-the-minute outfits as worn by the young ladies of the period.

Hair is styled with a center parting that has been left white

Molded side bows, with touches of gold paint, are a special feature

Hair is held in a snood at the back of the head

Eyebrows and upper lids are finely detailed in black paint

Shoulder head is sewn to body through holes in front and back of shoulder plate

Stitched seams form joints at shoulders

Overlarge hands: this body type was used to teach girls about human anatomy

Stuffed cloth arms

Torso is hand-seamed at the left side

Stitched seams at knees and hips allow limited movement

Cotton skirt and bodice, with frilled peplum at waist

Feet have no toes

C.1865 GERMAN DOLL WITH MARY HEAD
In the 1860s, wearing gilded hair bows was such a popular style with Mary Todd Lincoln – wife of President Abraham Lincoln – that doll heads showing her favorite coiffure are often named after her.

HT: 23in (58cm)

c.1840 GERMAN HEAD
(LEFT) *The high quality of this shoulder head is indicated by the delicately molded facial features; a fine red line that describes the curve of each eye socket; and the even blackness of the hair. Doll ht: 15in (38cm)*

Layers of overglaze give a deep, smooth sheen

PRESSED PORCELAIN (LEFT) *This*
c.1840 *German shoulder head is unusual in its flesh pink coloring. The hair, which shows rounded side panels covering the ears and a tightly knotted bun at the back of the head, is modeled after a style associated with the young English queen, Victoria. Head ht: 9in (23cm)*

Entire head is covered with a tinted underglaze

Front shoulder plate is slightly shaped to form a rounded bosom

Untinted head, with brightly painted, "rouged" cheeks

Wavy hair falls in loose curls and ringlets

Uneven thickness of the material indicates a pressed head

Brush-marked hair detail at sides of face

Painted eyes, with black upper lids and brick red shadow-line above

Sloping shoulder plate is sewn to a stuffed cloth torso

ONE OF A PAIR (ABOVE)
Although styled in the same way, the black coloring of this c.1865 *German lady's hair gives the doll a different appearance from that of its companion, shown in a back view below. Doll ht: 17½in (45cm)*

REAR VIEW (ABOVE) *As the* 19th *century progressed, plain hairstyles soon gave way to more elaborate models. These ringlets and braided, coiled bun belong to the* c.1850 *German doll at right. Ht: 4in (10cm)*

Different shades of color suggest fine hair texture

Tassels are adorned with a layer of lustrous gold paint

Hair is held loosely tucked up at the back of the head

GILDED SNOOD (LEFT)
Popular in the 1860s *and* 1870s, *snoods kept long hair neatly in place and decorated a lady's head at the same time. This one, seen on a* c.1865 *head, contains hair of a golden brown color, also known as café au lait. Doll ht: 12½in (32cm)*

c.1850 DRAPED HAIRSTYLE WITH RINGLETS (ABOVE)
Changing tastes softened the 1840s *sculptural "Queen Victoria" look into less severe styles. Few other changes were made to the doll, which still had the shoulder head attached by strong thread to a cloth body, often with kid arms. Ht: 16in (40cm)*

Plain Glazed China Heads

· 1840s to 1870s ·

SOME PORCELAIN DOLL HEADS are marked, but the maker is not known; others are unmarked. Where a mark exists, it often appears on the inside of the shoulder plate. Many of these heads are still sewn to their original bodies and cannot be examined, as damaging the threads to remove the head from the body would divest the doll of much of its historical and collectible value. Occasionally, a porcelain head is found that has never been used with a body. As so few makers have been identified, the information that can be gleaned from such heads makes them as valuable as complete dolls.

~ Not all doll heads were designed to show the ornate, elaborate hairstyles of fashionable ladies. Some have very simply modeled hair, with molded curls and painted feathering. These dolls with less decorative hairstyles generally portray boys, children, or babies.

Molded and painted hair, with side parting

Fine lines indicate upper eyelid and eye socket detail

Underglaze painted facial features

Closed mouth, colored orange, with darker shading between lips

Tape sewn around upper arms reinforces and hides the joins

Sleeves conceal glazed china arms, cast to above elbow

Oval blue ink stamp reads "Fr.H & CoJ/ Patent"

Binding around middle gives definition to the unshaped torso

Hands have molded, joined fingers and separate thumbs

Stitched seams at hips allow doll to sit securely on its rump

Painted pink garter band, tied in a bow

Clothing is from the doll's original wardrobe, part of which was bought at Izzard, a London toy store

Feet are shaped and painted to represent flat-heeled black ankle boots

Glazed china lower legs; left leg is a replacement of a slightly different size

Houndstooth check tweed trousers, with button-fly front

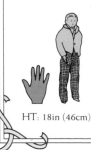

"ALLAN ALBERT" *This c.1861 glazed china shoulder head is sewn to a Fischer, Naumann and Co. stuffed cloth body. The front of the torso bears the ink stamp of Franz Haas and Co. Haas was probably the London sales agent for Fischer, Naumann, a German company. In 1860, Haas applied for a British patent for a cloth body that enabled the doll to sit.*

HT: 18in (46cm)

Very small head; hairstyle is that of a young man

Shoulder head is attached to a stuffed cloth torso and legs

High-quality pressed head is finely molded

The ink stamp, used c.1850, appears inside the shoulder plate. It shows a spread eagle encircled with the words "KOENIGL. PORZELLAN MANUFACTUR."

Molded hair, with feathered painting around the face

Flesh-colored tint covers the whole head

Sloping shoulders

HEAD OF A YOUTH

(ABOVE) The Königliche Porzellan Manufaktur is one of the few known makers of porcelain heads. This example of its design for a youth's head, made in the 1850s, is unfinished because of a firing flaw. Head ht: 5in (13cm)

BOY WITH LONG LEGS

(LEFT) With its elongated limbs and shoulder head measuring a mere 3in (7.5cm) high, this 1860s German doll has an odd but endearing appearance. The kid arms have hands shaped as fists, with no fingers or thumbs. Ht: 16in (40cm)

C.1865 GERMAN FLANGE NECK HEAD

(RIGHT) Relatively few flange neck heads were made: the majority of glazed china heads have shoulder plates. This example has molded blond curls rather than the usual head of dark hair. Its face is modeled to show the facial features of a baby. Ht: 6¼in (16cm)

Stuffed cloth upper limbs and torso

Doll wears its original clothes

Glazed china lower legs

Feet are molded to show joined toes

FLESH-TINTED HEAD (ABOVE)

Sometimes the same heads were used for dolls representing babies as well as older children. This c.1850 German head of an infant or child is marked with an "R" on the inside of the shoulder plate. Head ht: 3⅛in (8cm)

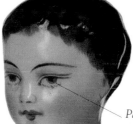

Painted cobalt blue eyes, with black pupils

Pressed shoulder head

RARE HEAD (ABOVE)

It is the coloring that makes this head unusual. it has purple-rose shadings above the eyes, below the mouth and at its corners, and on the ears; and the hair and eyebrows are dark brown — more common from the 1860s, but still less usual than black. It was made in the 1860s to late 1870s, probably in France. Doll ht: 9in (23cm)

Painted pale blue eyes

Cleft, slightly double, chin

Glazed china lower arms; fingers are curved toward palms

Informal smoking jacket, with wing-collared shirt and silk cravat

Hands are fists, with stitched fingers; stiff leather body

MINIATURE DOLL (RIGHT)

This diminutive figure of a young man, made in Germany c.1850s–1860s, has a flesh-tinted glazed china shoulder head. It is possibly a dolls' house doll. Underglaze painting gives the doll delicately rosy cheeks, violet blue and black eyes, and wispy locks of brown hair. Ht: 5in (13cm)

Fancy Untinted Bisque Heads

· 1860s to 1880s ·

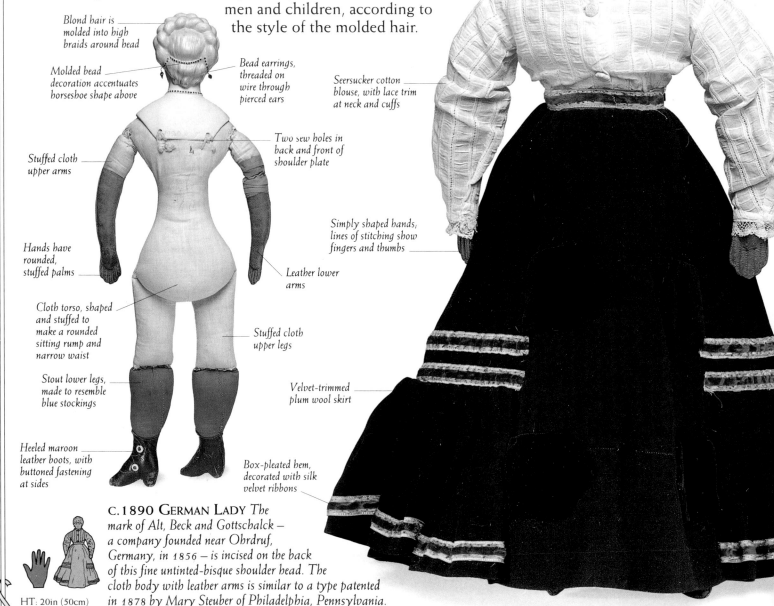

BY 1860, A MATTE PORCELAIN called untinted bisque began to replace glazed china. These later heads are sometimes also known as "parian," particularly in the United States, where the term has been used ever since the 1930s. "Parian" in fact refers to a variety of porcelain that was developed in the late 1840s by two English pottery factories, Minton and Copeland. This new porcelain, whose special properties gave it the luminous quality of white Parian marble, was probably never used for making doll heads, as it was very expensive to produce. The word "parian" did appear in many advertisements, perhaps as a sales ploy.
Untinted bisque heads lack the glossy finish of the glazed chinas, but are otherwise quite similar. They are usually white, except for the coloring of the facial features, and represent either ladies or men and children, according to the style of the molded hair.

Blue bead decoration is molded with the hair

Painted eyes, with black pupils and fine line below blue irises

Darker line between lips gives mouth slightly down-turned corners

Seersucker cotton blouse, with lace trim at neck and cuffs

Simply shaped hands; lines of stitching show fingers and thumbs

Velvet-trimmed plum wool skirt

Box-pleated hem, decorated with silk velvet ribbons

Blond hair is molded into high braids around head

Molded bead decoration accentuates horseshoe shape above

Bead earrings, threaded on wire through pierced ears

Two sew holes in back and front of shoulder plate

Stuffed cloth upper arms

Leather lower arms

Hands have rounded, stuffed palms

Cloth torso, shaped and stuffed to make a rounded sitting rump and narrow waist

Stuffed cloth upper legs

Stout lower legs, made to resemble blue stockings

Heeled maroon leather boots, with buttoned fastening at sides

C.1890 GERMAN LADY *The mark of Alt, Beck and Gottschalck — a company founded near Ohrdruf, Germany, in 1856 — is incised on the back of this fine untinted-bisque shoulder head. The cloth body with leather arms is similar to a type patented in 1878 by Mary Steuber of Philadelphia, Pennsylvania.*

HT: 20in (50cm)

Inset blue glass eyes, with black lashes and feathered blond brows

Pearl and gold bead earrings through pierced ears

Hair is molded to show looped curls

Copper luster finish on plume, giving it a metallic shine

1870s GERMAN GIRL (LEFT)

With its head marked "4 L 7," this doll is thought to be the work of C.F. Kling and Co. of Ohrdruf, Germany. The deep shoulder plate is sewn by three holes on either side to a stuffed cloth body.
Ht: 19in (48cm)

Leather lower arms; separate stitched fingers and thumbs

Hair is crimped into waves over forehead and curled and set in coils at back of head

Leather boots sewn to checked stockings form the lower legs

Unmarked German head, made late 1870s to early 1880s

UNTINTED BISQUE HEAD WITH MOLDED HAT (LEFT)

The chic molded hairstyles of lady doll heads were often adorned with trimmings, such as bows, or more elaborate confections. This 1860s German doll wears an elegant hat tipped low over a head of luxuriant blond hair. Doll ht: 10in (25cm)

Shoulder head is sewn to a stuffed cloth body, with bisque lower limbs; lower legs are molded to show flat-heeled boots

GERMAN HEAD WITH TIARA (LEFT)

Lusterware — porcelain with luster decoration — was greatly admired during the second half of the 19th century. Its popularity is reflected in the headdress of this delicately featured untinted bisque shoulder head, made c.1860.
Head ht: 5½in (14cm)

Gold earrings are painted onto ears

Molded black bow

Feathered eyebrows and painted lashes

Blond molded hair

Dress conceals stuffed cloth upper limbs and torso

Regional costume is hand-sewn

STYLISH REAR VIEW (RIGHT)

The back of a hairstyle can almost be more decorative than the front, as this immaculately presented 1870s coiffure shows. The German doll to which it belongs has an untinted bisque shoulder head on a cloth body.
Doll ht: 12in (30cm)

Pierced ears, with rosy lobes and gold earrings

Shoulders are tinted flesh pink

PATTERNED SHOULDER HEAD (LEFT)

This impressive example of porcelain molding and painting has thick braids of blond hair set high on the crown of the head, and two tiny kiss-curls to soften the forehead. Around the doll's throat is a black "velvet" neckband with a drop pendant. The tucked bodice sports ribbons, bows, and lace. Ht: 24in (60cm)

SIMON AND HALBIG LADY (RIGHT)

The mark "S 0 H" on the front of the shoulder plate identifies this head as one made by this famous firm. Inset glass eyes and bisque lower limbs, with the lower legs molded to show heeled boots and blue garter ribbons, all date the doll c.1870s. Ht: 12in (30cm)

Plain Untinted Bisque Heads

· 1860s to 1880s ·

UNTINTED BISQUE DOLL HEADS made around the end of the 1860s were often designed to show neat, flat hairstyles that were usually molded quite close to the crown, with a central part. Popularly known as flat-topped heads, most portray children or older boys. Heads that represent ladies were still produced, but in smaller quantities. Like the heads of the children and boys, the lady heads also show hairstyles that are far simpler than the crimped waves, exuberant curls, and coiled braids of the earlier models.

A noteworthy feature of the later dolls is the increasing use of bisque for the lower limbs, which are modeled in a fairly convincing manner. Particular attention was given to the legs, with the tiny feet molded and then painted to show fashionable boots.

Center parting is faintly indicated; no indent or white line

Painted blue eyes, with black pupils; light brown painted brows

Painted red mouth, with darker crossline and full lower lip

Inner eye corners and nostrils are highlighted with dots of red paint

Head is modeled to show a short, childlike neck and dimples beneath the collarbone

Two sew holes in front and back of shoulder plate

Doll wears a striped jacket over a coarse cotton undershirt

Hands have separate thumbs and inward-curving fingers

Cloth upper arms

Cloth upper legs and torso, shaped at waist; internal wire frame and sawdust stuffing

Bisque lower arms; thumbs show vertical casting lines

Stitching at joins between upper cloth and lower bisque legs allows the limbs to bend

Bisque lower legs are short and chunky, but well shaped

Breeches match the jacket

Painted boots on male dolls can have "elastic" at sides or "laced" fronts

Small heels — a post-1860 fashion style — help to date the doll

UNTINTED BISQUE HEAD WITH BISQUE LOWER LIMBS *The flowing blond curls of this c.1865 German shoulder head are typical of styles worn by young boys in the second half of the 19th century, when male children had long hair well beyond babyhood. The lower legs end in minute feet, shaped and decorated as fashionable heeled boots.*

Decorative lower legs

Painted pink garter ribbons

Purple-colored copper luster finish on ankle boots

HT: 10in (25cm)

Eyes lack socket lines and dots at corners

Poor-quality untinted bisque shoulder head

1860S BOY WITH FLAT BOOTS (LEFT) Poorer quality porcelain heads have a slightly grainy appearance and are sometimes described as "stoneware." The example shown here was made in Germany. Boots without heels were a popular style of footwear for both sexes before 1860. Ht: 9in (23cm)

Stuffed cloth upper limbs and torso

Curls extend around back of head

INTAGLIO EYES (RIGHT) The usual practice of molding painted eyes as convex shapes is reversed for intaglio eyes, which are concave – a style that was inherited from statuary carvings. Although intaglio eyes are a common feature of the later Gebrüder Heubach character heads, no other features of this German c.1870 untinted bisque shoulder head suggest that this famous firm was the maker. Doll ht: 15in (38cm)

Deep curls and ringlets

Eye sockets are heavily shadowed

Shoulder plate is molded as a blouse

1860S GERMAN HEAD (LEFT) A slight irregularity in the facial features adds a charming naïveté to this untinted bisque shoulder head. Its mouth is finely modeled, with the somewhat downturned corners of a child's face in repose. Doll ht: 17in (43cm)

Bisque lower arms; hands are simply modeled

SCOTS BOY (BELOW) With its molded hair painted brown, this costume doll possibly dates between 1870 and 1875: hair colored either brown or blond may indicate a later head. The eyes are molded to show heavy lids over large black pupils and pale blue irises. Ht: 8½in (22cm)

Shoulders slope sharply away from the neck

Painted flat-heeled boots

Ceramic lower legs, cast to above knees

C.1875 SWIVEL HEAD (RIGHT) Representing a young girl, this swivel head was probably made by the famous German doll manufacturer Simon and Halbig. It has especially striking, luminous dark blue painted eyes, framed by black lashes and feathered eyebrows. The full, orange-red lips, separated by a crimson crossline, almost appear to smile. Doll ht: 9in (23cm)

Feathered, light brown eyebrows

Pale red mouth, with darker highlights

Feathered eyebrows follow the shape of the eye sockets

Inset blue glass eyes

Painted black upper and lower eyelashes

Rosebud mouth

Hands have stitched fingers and separate thumbs

Neck fits into the separately cast shoulder plate, allowing head to turn

LADY WITH GLASS EYES (RIGHT) The hair of this c.1870s shoulder head is styled into rows of ringlets and deep fronds over the forehead that provide a nice balance to the head's square jaw. Delicately painted facial features complement the doll's deep blue glass eyes. Doll ht: 12in (30cm)

Molded and painted tassel

Heel and boot upper are painted to look like leather

BISQUE DETAIL (LEFT) The Lady with Glass Eyes at left has a stuffed cloth torso and upper limbs, and lower limbs of bisque. The lower legs are molded and painted to show gaiter-type boots, with a scalloped side-button fastening. Worn by young women of the smart set, they have toes designed to fit only the daintiest of fashionably small feet.

Sporran is made of horse or deer hair

Bisque Dolls

Doll language gives the name "bisque" to a type of porcelain that has been fired twice, with color added – both as an overall tint and as detailed highlights – before the second firing. The difference between bisque heads and other porcelain types lies in the finish: though glazed, bisque does not have the glossy sheen of the glazed chinas; neither has it the matte texture and marblelike whiteness of most untinted bisque heads.

BISQUE BECAME AN INCREASINGLY POPULAR material for doll heads in the mid-nineteenth century, and it remained so until the 1930s. Bisque heads were expensive to make, but if produced in large quantities, could be cost-effective. Many of the German factories that produced bisque heads, limbs, and complete dolls were already manufacturing porcelain or earthenware household items. Some were almost cottage industries, with only a single kiln. Others were much larger, having workshops covering several acres. Most were in Thuringia, a region in eastern Germany that had abundant supplies of raw clay and wood. Cheap labor was available, too.

〜 To make a bisque head, a clay mixture was cast in a two- or three-part, usually plaster,

mold. The molds were carefully scrutinized prior to the casting, as any flaws would be reproduced in the castings. Each mold was used only 40 or 50 times before it was discarded. Early heads were made of a stiff clay "paste" pressed into the molds; later, a pourable, semi-liquid clay slip was perfected. This slip produced heads with a smoother surface and allowed greater refinement in the modeling of facial features than was possible using the pressed material.

〜 When firmly set, the doll head or other part (called greenware in its prefired state) was removed from the mold. The casting lines were cleaned, it was fired, colored, and fired again. The heads needed special supports while in the kilns, because they

C.1870 BÉBÉ JUMEAU (LEFT)
Finding a famous-name, marked doll, with its original clothing and packaging, is a real joy. This bébé has a pressed bisque head and a composition and wood body, stamped "BÉBÉ JUMEAU Bte. S.G.D.G. DÉPOSÉ." Ht: 31in (80cm)

POST-1910 INDIAN GIRL
(RIGHT) *This charming figure is one of Simon and Halbig's "Dolls of Four Races." Its bisque socket head, composition body, flirty glass eyes, and human hair wig are all colored to represent a girl from India. Ht: 12in (30cm)*

WALTERSHAUSEN WORKSHOP

(LEFT) *Kämmer and Reinhardt was founded in 1886 by doll designer Ernst Kämmer and salesman Franz Reinhardt. The left-hand side of the photograph at left shows the painting of doll heads at one of its workshops in Waltershausen, Germany, using a new technique developed by the company. The right-hand side of the photograph shows the making of human hair eyelashes. This was also a Kämmer and Reinhardt innovation.*

ASSEMBLING THE DOLLS

(LEFT) *Another photograph taken in one of Kämmer and Reinhardt's Waltershausen workshops shows a selection of bisque heads and composition bodies, ready to be put together. The finishing of the dolls was always done in the factory, but outworkers were hired for other parts of the production process, such as making the blown glass eyes. Kämmer and Reinhardt produced numerous doll designs, including a successful line of character dolls.*

C.1897 GIRL (ABOVE) *This J.D. Kestner doll has what is known as a "bald head." Beneath the wig, the pate has not been cut away for the insertion of the eyes. Ht. 18in (46cm)*

were liable to sag on their necks when water in the porcelain slip evaporated during the initial firing.

The first heads made had molded hair and eyes, and closed mouths. Later heads have glass eyes, either inset, or the lead-weighted sleeping or flirty type. For these, the eye sockets were cut out and shaped at the greenware stage. Molded ears, teeth, and tongues were usually designed as part of the mold, but inset teeth (produced in quantity by the Simon and Halbig company) were made separately and glued into the mouth before the final dressing of the head.

Investigating the Facts

Today, there is some confusion about where and when bisque doll heads were made, and by whom. Many of the incised marks on bisque heads are unclear, and some trademarks, too, are often very similar to one another, making it hard to identify the true maker. What *is* known is that far more bisque doll heads were produced in Thuringia than anywhere else. The production of some French factories, such as Jumeau and Steiner, is also well documented, and it is probable that German firms occasionally met the production needs of French factories whose output was oversubscribed. Large numbers of bisque heads were

exported and attached to their "foreign" bodies later: a German head on a French body, dressed in England, for example, is still considered to be an original doll. Nowadays, a doll's country of origin is given as the country in which its head was made, as it is in the head that the doll's "personality" is conveyed.

There is little doubt that France and Germany dominated the international market for bisque doll heads, limbs, and complete dolls until 1914, when World War I interrupted their manufacturing. England produced rather poor quality stoneware, as opposed to porcelain, doll parts; and dolls from Japan, though made of porcelain, fell far below the very high standards set by France and Germany.

1920S ENGLISH STONEWARE HEAD (RIGHT) *Glass eyes were usually inserted into ceramic heads by cutting away the crown, setting the eyes, and then replacing the cut section with a piece of cork – a very neat operation that was completely concealed beneath the doll's wig. Head ht. 4in (10cm)*

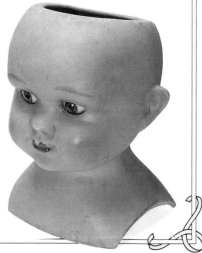

Fashionable Lady Dolls

· 1860s to 1890s ·

FASHION DOLLS – stylish representations of elegant young ladies in *haute couture* – were at their most popular between 1860 and 1890. Although most came from France, many were merely assembled there, using swivel heads or shoulder heads imported from German porcelain makers on French-made bodies. While many heads are unmarked, and others bear figures or characters that are not identified as the marks of any known maker, it is thought that some well-known French factories, such as Jumeau and Bru, did produce bisque heads.

Dolls of this type usually have inset (rarely sleeping) oval or almond-shaped glass eyes. Their stuffed kid bodies are skilfully pieced together in sections to recreate the undulating curves of a young woman wearing a tightly laced, boned corset.

Ash blonde mohair wig (a modern replacement) is pinned to the original cork pate

Painted eyebrows and lashes

Inset glass eyes are pale blue, with a darker outer rim

Pierced ears

Closed mouth

Sleeves conceal shoulder plate, marked "4" on the edge

Original strawberry blonde mohair wig

Inset brown glass eyes are a striking feature; blue eyes are usual

Pale bisque swivel head, with typically long face and full cheeks

Elbows have V-shaped gussets so that arms can bend

Stuffed kid arms, torso, and legs, in excellent condition

Top of kid torso is glued over the bisque shoulder plate

Arms, legs, and torso are made of firmly stuffed kid

Hands have separate fingers and thumbs

Thumbs and fingers are separate

On back of doll: large gussets between rump and upper thighs allow limited movement

Stockings, pinned to legs, cover gussets at backs of knees

Sawdust-stuffed body; internal wire frame gives support

Striped silk dress, with heavy velvet collar and sleeve trim

Sewn-on shoes hide simply shaped feet

C.1875 FRENCH LADIES At 33cm (13in) high, the undressed doll shown here is somewhat shorter than its dressed companion, though the two are otherwise quite similar. Their bisque swivel heads have socket necks set into the bisque shoulder plates, which allow the heads to be attractively angled.

HT: 46cm (18in)

Inset large blue-gray glass eyes

Closed mouth

SUMMER OUTFIT (LEFT) The rounded face and sweetly innocent facial expression of this c.1875 French Belton-type shoulder head indicate that the doll was intended to represent a young girl rather than a lady. It sports the pierced ears — here threaded with blue bead earrings — seen on most of the fashion dolls. Ht: 15in (38cm)

Gusseted kid arms, torso, and legs

Simple cotton outfit, topped with a flower-trimmed straw hat, suits the doll's childlike appearance

UNDERGARMENTS A LA MODE (RIGHT) Attributed to Margueritte Frène of Caen, France, this bisque shoulder head dates from the late 1870s. The doll has two rare features: the vibrant coloring of the cheeks; and the closed, upturned "smiling" mouth. Ht: 26in (65cm)

Chestnut brown human hair wig

Painted chin highlights echo those of the cheeks

Stuffed kid arms, with gussets at elbows

Separate fingers and thumbs

Period undergarments cover the stuffed kid body and legs; gussets at hips and knees

Flat-soled feet have separate toes

FOOTWEAR FOR LADIES (BELOW) The fine accessories of fashion dolls were handcrafted with as much attention to detail as the real-life items they copied. These tiny leather shoes are for cloth or kid feet. Dolls with bisque lower legs have molded and painted feet to suggest boots.

c.1875 leather shoe, with high back and buttoned ankle strap

Molded bisque gaiter-type boot, with tassel top; foot detail of lady at right

Post-1875 pink-tinted bisque shoulder head

Inset blue glass eyes; fine lines radiate from pupils to edges of irises

TEA ON THE LAWN (RIGHT) Dolls with heads that turn and movable limbs have great appeal. This 1870s French lady has a bisque swivel head. The hips and knees have V-shaped gussets that allow the limbs to be placed in a variety of positions. Ht: 12½in (32cm)

Silk and lace parasol, with brass fittings

Ostrich feathers, dyed blue to match stripes in dress

Inset blue glass eyes have very large pupils

Promenade dress, made of net woven with stripes of blue satin

Bisque lower arms; hands have joined fingers and separate thumbs

Pale pink bisque lower arms

Dress conceals sawdust-filled cotton body

GIRL WITH PAINTED BOOTS (RIGHT) Made in France after 1875, this doll is thought to have been created by doll-maker Huret. The short dress indicates that the doll represents a girl rather than a lady. A detail of the doll's bisque lower leg is shown in close-up above. Ht: 19in (48cm)

Close-up of boot is shown above

Developments in Body Types

· 1860s to 1880s ·

THE 20 YEARS BETWEEN 1860 and 1880 were halcyon days for the fashionably dressed dolls of France and Germany, and manufacturers ensured their continuing popularity by making increasingly realistic bodies for the dolls' fine bisque heads. Bisque lower arms and sometimes legs replaced stuffed kid limbs, and though early models are clumsy compared to the delicately stitched kid, later castings are more refined. The articulation of doll bodies was a new challenge, and it was here that the greatest advances were made. The French firm Gesland operated in Paris from 1860 to 1928. The jointed metal frame of its padded stockinette body allowed the limbs and torso to assume and retain a variety of positions, and was a major innovation of this particular period.

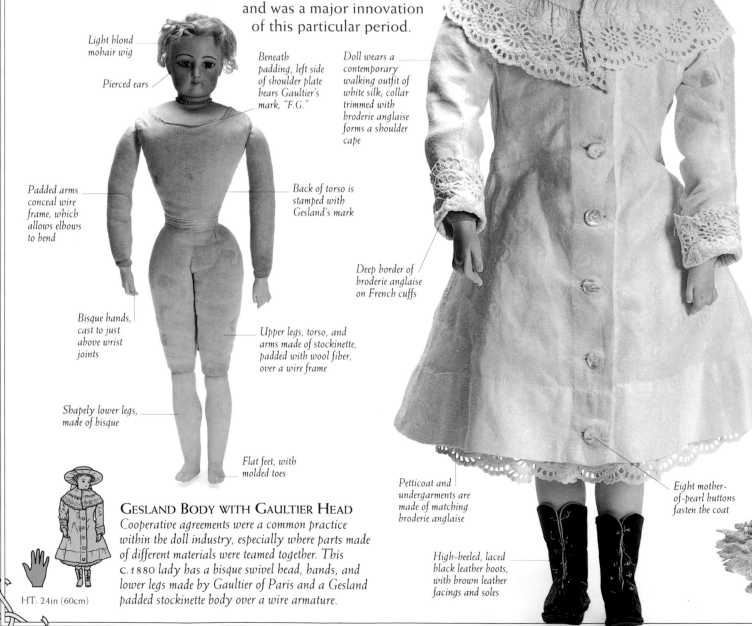

Light blond mohair wig

Pierced ears

Beneath padding, left side of shoulder plate bears Gaultier's mark, "F.G."

Doll wears a contemporary walking outfit of white silk; collar trimmed with broderie anglaise forms a shoulder cape

Swivel head can be turned on its shoulder plate

Padded arms conceal wire frame, which allows elbows to bend

Back of torso is stamped with Gesland's mark

Bisque hands, cast to just above wrist joints

Upper legs, torso, and arms made of stockinette, padded with wool fiber, over a wire frame

Deep border of broderie anglaise on French cuffs

Shapely lower legs, made of bisque

Flat feet, with molded toes

Petticoat and undergarments are made of matching broderie anglaise

Eight mother-of-pearl buttons fasten the coat

High-heeled, laced black leather boots, with brown leather facings and soles

GESLAND BODY WITH GAULTIER HEAD

Cooperative agreements were a common practice within the doll industry, especially where parts made of different materials were teamed together. This c.1880 lady has a bisque swivel head, hands, and lower legs made by Gaultier of Paris and a Gesland padded stockinette body over a wire armature.

HT: 24in (60cm)

White
mohair wig

Long, waisted
jacket of
purple silk,
with square
scallop detail
at hem

Kid hands have
well-shaped,
separate fingers
and thumbs

Original
striped silk
skirt, showing
damage by
sunlight

BISQUE-HEADED TWINS (RIGHT)
Probably of German origin, this pair was
made toward the end of the 1870s. The
naked figure is a fine example of a kid doll
body of the late 1800s. Other materials
were also available, but high-quality bodies
were usually made of kid.
Ht: 18in (46cm)

Torso, upper arms,
and legs are made
of wood covered
with kid

Joints at
hips, so doll
can sit easily

Inset blue glass
eyes, with painted
lashes and brows

Tenon
joints at
elbows
and waist

Joints at ankles and knees
for optimum movement

Bisque swivel
head

Promenade
costume,
made of silk

Bisque
lower
arms

Thick mohair
wig dressed in
braids, pinned
to a cork pate

Close-fitting,
short-waisted
jacket, with
flared sleeves

Bustle and
train at
back of
skirt

Flat fronted
skirt: a late
1870s style

C.1866 "MANUELITA"
(ABOVE) This elegant French lady
doll has a body of stuffed kid and a
pale bisque swivel head, with inset
almond-shaped dark blue glass eyes,
and a mohair wig. Ht: 15in (38cm)

Brown mohair wig
over a cork pate

Shoulder plate is
molded to show a
high bosom

V-shaped
gussets at
elbows

Finely made
kid hands, with
long fingers

Elaborate, two-
tiered train, edged
with checked
quilting
and lace

Lower eye
sockets have dark
painted rims

THE BRIDE (LEFT) Fashion dolls
are unrivaled in displaying the styles
of the period. Here, a doll with a
French or German bisque shoulder
head and kid body models an 1880s
bridal gown. Ht: 14in (35cm)

C.1870 BARROIS LADY (RIGHT) The
mark "E. Déposé B.," which is incised on
this doll's front shoulder plate, is that of
E. Barrois. Porcelain factories in both
France and Germany produced heads
for this famous Parisian company
between 1844 and 1877.
Ht: 12½in (32cm)

Lace-trimmed, cream
satin gown, with pleats,
bows, and flounces

Arched feet
have toes
indicated
with lines
of stitching

Satin-trimmed
muslin skirt over
a hooped crinoline

Bisque
shoulder head

Closed mouth

Blond fleece
wig, with
skin backing

Inset azure blue
glass eyes

Dress conceals
stuffed kid
upper arms,
torso, and legs

Bisque lower
arms, with
molded fingers
and thumbs

Jumeau Dolls

· 1842 to 1958 ·

PIERRE FRANÇOIS JUMEAU established his company in Paris in 1842, originally making wood or kid doll bodies and doll clothes. In 1867, his son, Emile, joined the firm, bringing a fresh spirit of commercial enterprise. The company expanded, and in 1873 began to make bisque doll heads, cast at its factory outside Paris in Montreuil-sous-Bois. Soon after, Emile introduced the *bébés Jumeau* – dolls with fine bisque heads, jointed composition bodies, and an innocent expression. Their quality and appeal did much to establish Jumeau's reputation. ∾ Faced with increasing competition from German doll-makers, Jumeau amalgamated with other French companies in 1899 to form the *Société Française de Fabrication de Bébés et Jouets* (S.F.B.J.). Both name and company survived within the *Société* until trading came to an end in 1958.

Matching velvet bonnet, trimmed with dyed ostrich feathers

Inset pale blue glass eyes; fine lines radiating from pupils give lifelike effect

Lower eyelashes are detailed with precise brushstrokes

Dark blond mohair wig, curled into corkscrews over forehead

Bisque socket head

Rosebud mouth, deeply indented; darker highlights accentuate the fine molding of the lips

Long silk tunic dress, with silk checked collar

Wood and composition arms, ball-jointed at elbows and shoulders

Marked composition torso, molded to show a rounded belly and chest

Childlike, chubby hands, with short fingers and thumbs

Doll wears its original outfit, a tunic dress; front facings form two false pockets at hem

Composition legs, with ball joints at knees and hips

Whole body is varnished over five layers of flesh-tone paint

Pleated silk "skirt," trimmed with lace

Petticoat is edged with handmade lace

Long toes are molded together, but still well defined

Machine-knitted socks, made of mercerized cotton

Faded maroon leather shoes are stamped on soles "EJUMEAU/ MED OR/ 1876/ PARIS/DÉPOSÉ"

Silk rosettes match the rest of the doll's outfit

BÉBÉ JUMEAU *The inspiration for the bébés Jumeau is said to have come from a portrait of Henri IV of France, aged four. Whatever the source, their insouciant charm has won the hearts of buyers and collectors since the first doll was sold. This example dates from between 1880 and 1885, and shows the exceptionally fine quality of Jumeau dolls manufactured before 1899.*

HT: 22in (55cm)

Strawberry blond mohair wig

Large inset blue glass eyes

White line suggests a row of teeth

Pierced ears

"FLORENCE" (RIGHT)
Named by her original child owner, "Florence" is a large bébé of late 1880s or early 1890s vintage. Like all the bébés, the doll has a bisque socket head and a papier-mâché composition body, jointed at the shoulders, elbows, hips, and knees so that the limbs can be moved into various positions. The head and body are both marked (see Doll Marks, right).
Ht: 30in (75cm)

Salmon pink velvet dress is a later purchase; dolls were often sold unclothed

Cork pate fits snugly into head cavity

Glass eyes inserted through cut section

Socket head turns easily to either side

HEAD PROFILE (ABOVE)
Carefully removing the mohair wig from the head of "Florence" reveals the cork pate to which it was pinned – a method of attaching hair that was used for most Jumeau dolls. The profile also shows two other features: the realistic modeling of the molded ears, and the bulbous, luminous blown glass eyes (sometimes called paperweight eyes).

DOLL MARKS
These ink stamps are from the doll "Florence"; they are usually found together.

~

Patented head details include the size: "14" indicates a height of 30in (75cm).

> DÉFOSÉ
> TÊTE JUMEAU
> B^tSGDG
> 14

Body mark refers to the 1885 Paris Exhibition – the doll was awarded the gold medal.

> JUMEAU
> MÉDAILLE D'OR
> PARIS

C.1875 FASHION DOLL (LEFT)
Though unmarked, this doll is of a type also associated with Jumeau. Its bisque swivel head, with inset glass eyes, pierced ears, and blond mohair wig, and its gusseted, stuffed kid, internally wired body are common features of fashion dolls made from 1860 to 1880. The doll wears a silk walking outfit and side-buttoning leather boots in period style.
Ht: 14in (35cm)

The bee trade-mark, stamped on the soles of some doll shoes made by Jumeau, was registered in 1891.

> PARIS
> DÉPOSÉ

Blond mohair wig, styled in ringlets

Inset pale blue glass eyes

Fingers of right hand are curved to hold a parasol

FRENCH NURSEMAID (LEFT)
This mechanical doll has an unmarked bisque swivel head, probably made by Jumeau between 1880 and 1890. Inside its body is a Roullet and Decamps wind up mechanism, which is wound with a key projecting from the doll's right hip. The nursemaid and mailcart – the vehicle holding the baby – are joined together, allowing the entire ensemble to move forward as the doll "walks."
Ht: 12in (30cm)

Fringed silk canopy, now very worn

Baby is all-bisque, jointed at shoulders and hips

Bent arms, with hands shaped as fists

Metal mailcart – a type of stroller

Stockings conceal bisque lower legs

Bisque lower legs, molded and painted to show heeled boots

Bru Dolls

· 1866 to 1950s ·

IN 1866, THE FRENCH FIRM Bru Jne. and Cie. appeared as a strong contender for supremacy in the bisque doll marketplace, seriously rivaling the products of the other up-and-coming manufacturer in France, Jumeau (see pages 58–59). Casimir Bru Jeune (Junior) was the firm's first proprietor, followed by H. Chevrot in 1883, and Paul Eugène Girard seven years later. In 1899, Bru became a member of the new *Société Française de Fabrication de Bébés et Jouets* (S.F.B.J.), which produced dolls using original Bru molds until the 1950s.

Both before and after joining the *Société*, Bru produced a host of different models, among them mechanical dolls, such as its own type of *bébé baiser* or kiss-throwing doll. Most Brus have swivel, socket, or shoulder heads made of bisque; fleece, mohair, or human hair wigs; glass eyes; and pierced ears.

Pressed felt hat, trimmed with matching silk ribbon; outfits of dolls that were sold fully clothed usually included headwear

Blond fleece wig is pinned to the cork pate beneath

Large inset brown glass eyes

Pierced ears

Open/closed mouth, molded and painted to show tongue and teeth

Double-breasted wool jacket, with linen shirt and fabric-covered buttons

Bisque swivel head; dot within a circle is incised on back

Pink-tinged nipples are indicated in the front shoulder plate

Stuffed kid upper arms

Kid torso is firmly padded, with a rounded belly

Bisque lower arms

Knuckles are tinted with flesh tones

Hands have partly joined fingers and separate thumbs

Stuffed kid upper legs

At back, gussets between rump and tops of thighs allow upper legs to bend

Fingernails are indented, with red paint detail at base

Gussets at knees allow lower legs to bend

Stuffed kid lower legs

Toes are indicated with stitching

Knee-length wool breeches match the jacket

Machine-knitted socks, with scalloped tops

BÉBÉ BRU *The most sought after of all the bébés Bru are those with kid bodies. Made between 1872 and 1954, the bébés could be purchased naked; partly dressed, in chemise and drawers; or fully clothed. This c.1880 doll wears the costume of a sailor boy, but could represent a girl child equally well, as two dresses and petticoats form part of its original wardrobe.*

Glacé leather, flat-heeled boots

HT: 15in (38cm)

New mohair wig, pinned to the original cork pate

Open/closed mouth

Finely modeled right hand

Glass eyes may have been reset

Ball joints at shoulders

C.1890 BRU GIRL (LEFT)
Illustrating another style of body designed by Bru, this doll has a bisque swivel head and shoulder plate incised "BRU JNE/8." Heads on kid-and-composition bodies often bear this type of mark, which may also be found on heads used with gusseted kid bodies. Ht: 22in (55cm)

Upper arms of kid over wood-and-composition

Hinged elbow joints

Bisque lower arms

Hidden mortise and tenon joints at hips

Kid over wood-and-composition upper legs and torso

Lower legs made of painted composition

DOLL MARKS
Swivel heads have corresponding marks incised on the neck and shoulder plate.

Leather boots and shoes made for Bru dolls may be stamped with the maker's name inside an oval.

Bisque swivel head; incised on nape of neck "Bru Jne/6"

Heavily painted eyebrows, a special Bru feature

Titian mohair wig

Inset blue glass eyes

1880s GIRL CHILD (LEFT)
This pert faced bébé Bru has the same head and body as the sailor boy opposite, with a mohair, rather than fleece, wig. The practice of replacing wigs was once quite common among collectors who did not like the makers' original designs. Ht: 18in (46cm)

Silk costume is in period style but not original to doll

Delicate bisque lower arms, a feature of Bru dolls

C.1890 "SERENA"
(RIGHT) The owner of this Bru girl has kept the doll intact – it is all original and has no replacement parts. It has a bisque swivel head and shoulder plate, large inset brown glass eyes, and a long ash blond mohair wig. The lace that borders the dress was handmade by a nanny in Ayrshire, Scotland. Ht: 20in (50cm)

HEAD PROFILE (ABOVE)
Along with other makers of the period, Bru made its own style of lady doll between 1866 and 1870s. These dolls have bisque shoulder or – as here – swivel heads, usually teamed with stuffed kid bodies. They may also be called "smilers," after their main feature: a small mouth, with the lips pursed into a tight smile. Ht: 16in (40cm)

Clothes cover a kid over wood-and-composition body and composition legs

Bronze leather ankle-strap shoes, with matching ribbon bows on toes

Lady with Bru Wooden Body

· 1870s ·

A VARIETY OF DIFFERENT STYLES OF DOLL were made during the 1870s, as companies vied with each other to produce the very best models showing the most innovative designs. Dolls that could walk, talk, throw kisses, or even do all three at once, found eager buyers; but against all the competition, a model of enduring popularity emerged: the doll with a fine bisque swivel head and matching shoulder plate attached to a shapely body. Many attempts were made to create the ideal body – this objective proved elusive until the development of the fully jointed types. In 1872, Bru Jne. and Cie. issued a product catalog listing doll bodies made of stuffed kid or a combination of kid and wood. It also included a marvelous new design – an all-wooden lady doll body (quite similar to the one shown here) resembling an artist's manniquin, and using two different varieties of joint to provide maximum movement for the limbs.

Reddish blond human hair wig

Closed mouth; darker paint detail highlights bow of the lips

Bisque swivel head, lightly tinted to resemble fine white skin

Neck socket is lined with kid, to prevent chafing as head turns

Inset blue glass eyes

Band of kid covers the join between bisque shoulder plate and wooden torso

Mortise and tenon joints at shoulders

Cotton chemise top; front fastens with cotton-covered buttons

Flange joints allow lower arms to rotate

Mortise and tenon joints at elbows

Wooden parts are painted flesh pink and varnished

Mortise and tenon joints at hips

Wooden torso, carved to show narrow waist, buxom hips, and flattened bosom

Flaking paint exposes bare wood beneath

Ball and socket joints at wrists

Boned cotton twill corset, shaped to the doll's torso

Longish, nicely rounded thighs

Flange joints at mid-upper legs, so lower legs can rotate

Mortise and tenon joints at knees

Bottoms of feet are arched between ankles and toes

Split drawers with open crotch, made in one piece with the chemise

C.1870 ARTICULATED LADY *This elegant, carved wooden body, designed specifically for lady dolls, re-creates the "ideal" look of the 1870s, when a rounded body with small waist was considered the most attractive female shape. Compared to the curvaceous torso, the doll's limbs appear rather unrefined, though the feet are surprisingly detailed.*

HT: 22in (55cm)

Deep notches separate the toes

Delicately modeled feet

Rounded lid provides
extra space for topmost
items packed inside

Parchment paper and
"ivory" fan, painted
with white edelweiss

Lace-trimmed satin
peignoir – a type of
dressing gown

TRAVELING BOX (LEFT) The
lady's wardrobe of fashionable
outfits, undergarments, and
accessories is conveniently housed
inside a Saratoga trunk – a round-
lidded case frequently used by ladies
when traveling. This miniature
replica of a full-sized trunk is made
of wood covered in leather cloth,
with leather bindings and metal
fittings. A removable tray (see
below) fits snugly within the body
of the trunk. The lining paper is
printed with brightly colored
candy stripes – a favorite late
19th-century design.

Feather-stitching
attaches the lace trim

Pretty short-sleeved
summer dress, made
of printed muslin

Strap
secured to
lid and base

Metal carrying
handles at sides

Back view of doll's corset,
with laced eyelet fastening

Wicker jewelry box,
base is lined with cotton

Embossed
"silver" pendant
necklet

"Pearl" and
"jet" necklaces

Pink and black bead
necklace, with bead drops

LIFT-OUT TRAY (BELOW) The
more fragile items and those that
might damage the clothing are
kept in the trunk's removable
tray. Stored in the front
section are (left to right) two
pairs of leather walking boots;
stoppered glass bottles for perfume
and toilet waters; a leather purse;
diamanté jewelry on a satin reticule;
and a mirror with filigree back.

Straw hat, with braided
brim and chiffon trim

Black lace and
ribbon trim

Bonnet with ostrich
feathers and ruched silk

LADY AT LEISURE (BELOW)
Writing letters was a popular
pastime of wealthy young ladies
in the 19th century. They would
correspond about society, clothes,
music, dancing, their travels,
families, and their latest beaux.

Bone-handled umbrella,
with cotton cover
and metal fittings

Handmade
writing paper

Matching
envelopes, tied with
original silk ribbon

Elbow-length
kid gloves

Mirror-backed
wooden hairbrush

Kid gloves

Tortoise-shell
lorgnette

French miniature
pocket watch

Wooden hairbrush,
with real bristles

Tortoise-shell comb

Cotton
parasol, with
wooden handle

Steiner Dolls

· 1855 to 1908 ·

JULES NICHOLAS STEINER is probably better remembered for his company's wonderful mechanical dolls than for their intricate wind-up movements, which he also designed. A former clockmaker, Steiner founded the Steiner Société (also known as Steiner Cie.) in 1855. The company survived his death in 1891 and continued to trade until 1908, yet it was undoubtedly Steiner who provided the creative impetus for this Parisian business; during his leadership, the firm won several prizes. Along with the complex, expensive mechanical dolls, the Steiner Société produced simpler models and nonmechanical play dolls. All have bisque heads, which are thought to have been made in French porcelain factories, although the heads of the mechanical dolls rarely bear any company's mark.

Lace-trimmed silk bonnet, tied with silk velvet ribbons

Inset deep blue glass eyes

Open mouth, showing four teeth at top and bottom

Rosy pink tint on fingernails

White silk floss wig, pinned to a cork pate

Unmarked pale bisque shoulder head

Heavy metal armature at shoulders, for moving the arms

Upper arms of kid stretched over pressed cardboard

Kid-covered wooden torso ends at waist

Bisque lower arms are cast to well above elbows

Bisque lower arms, robustly modeled

Pasteboard bell forms the lower half of the doll

Metal frame within bell houses and protects the wind-up mechanism

Brass winding key

Printed cotton dress is designed to conceal the doll's working parts

Wooden base

Rivets attach the pasteboard bell to the base

1870S AUTOMATED LADY *The mechanism inside this doll is wound with a brass key and is activated by an on–off switch next to the key. The wheel can be set so the doll rotates or moves forward, simultaneously raising and lowering its arms and calling, "Mama!"*

HT: 15in (38cm)

Rotating wheel

Label of London doll-maker and seller Charles Marsh (see page 35)

On–off switch

Winding key

BASE DETAIL (LEFT) The three small wheels that protrude through the holes cut in the Automated Lady's wooden base have three separate functions: one stabilizes the doll; one is the drive wheel; and one sets its direction.

Stabilizer wheel

Drive wheel

STEINER KICKING DOLL

(BELOW) An unusual feature of the dressed doll pictured at bottom is revealed in this detail: a bisque head with flange neck, which fits over the metal bar that turns the head from side to side. The doll's inset deep blue glass eyes and open, toothed mouth are typical of Steiner automata.

DOLL MARKS

Mechanical dolls may be marked only on the wind-up mechanism itself.

The paper label on post-1889 dolls details the name, patent registration, and award date.

ARRESTED MOVEMENT (LEFT and BELOW) The Kicker – seen here in "action" – found a popular market in the United States and Europe between 1870 and 1890. The wind-up mechanism that controls its head, arms, and legs also enables the doll to utter a plaintive cry. Ht: 18in (46cm)

Mohair wig, styled with side parting

Inset large blue glass eyes

Closed mouth

Heavy, feathered eyebrows

Bisque socket head, incised at back below hairline "J. STEINER/ BTE S.G.D.G./PARIS/ FiRE A 9"

Composition arms, jointed at shoulders and elbows

Label reads "LE PETIT PARISIEN/ BÉBÉ J.STEINER/ MARQUE DÉPOSÉE/ MÉDAILLE D'OR/ PARIS/1889"

Typical feature: fingers are all roughly the same length

Composition upper legs and torso, jointed at hips

Composition lower legs, jointed at knees

Space between big and smaller toes

Unjointed composition arms

Kid and composition torso

Torso houses the doll's mechanism

Head turns from side to side as doll moves

Beneath dress, key and lever activate the wind-up mechanism

Blond mohair wig, with flat top and curls

Composition lower legs

Splay-toed feet are designed for kicking, rather than walking

POST-1890 BÉBÉ STEINER

(ABOVE) Steiner bébés are usually characterized by their pretty faces, with closed mouths and heavily painted eyebrows. Their bisque socket heads usually bear one of the Steiner marks incised on the nape of the neck Ht: 15in (38cm)

The S.F.B.J. and Others

· 1899 to 1950s ·

DURING THE FINAL DECADES of the nineteenth century, more and more German dolls were imported into France, presenting a lively threat to the already competitive home market. Ten companies responded to this disquieting development by forming, in 1899, the *Société Française de Fabrication de Bébés et Jouets* (S.F.B.J.) – a union composed largely of French doll producers, including both Jumeau and Bru. Some German companies were also admitted, notably the country's largest single investor, Fleischmann and Bloedel.

~ In 1905, the S.F.B.J. registered its trademark: a circle divided into quarters, each segment containing one of the *Société's* four initials. Other marks on S.F.B.J. dolls use the same initials, with mold and size numbers.

S.F.B.J. dolls made after 1905 often have this printed paper label stuck to their bodies. The details on the label are usually repeated in the incised head marks.

Shoulder-length mohair wig, styled with a left-side parting

Pierced ears

Bisque socket head

Ball joints at wrists allow hands to rotate

Composition hands; separately molded fingers and thumbs

Composition legs

Roughly modeled feet: toes are barely distinguished

Silk hat with upturned brim; doll outfits usually included matching headwear

Top eyelashes are made of animal hair

Open mouth, with a row of molded top teeth, is characteristic of S.F.B.J. dolls

Composition arms, jointed at elbows

At back of torso, paper label is stuck to the left side

Composition body, jointed at hips and shoulders

Ball joints at knees give lower legs backward and sideways movement

Sleeping brown glass eyes; single-color eyes are an S.F.B.J. feature

Bottom eyelashes are painted

Dress is made from a lightweight fabric known as "washing silk"

Book bound in tooled leather is a tiny replica of a 1903 German diary

Wickerwork valise, with bound cane handles

Machine-crocheted cotton socks

Simple mercerized cotton ties

Cloth shoes, with cardboard-reinforced soles

C.1905 S.F.B.J. GIRL *Although many of the firms that joined the Société were renowned for the excellence of their products, dolls manufactured under the S.F.B.J. blanket were usually of a poorer quality. This early model, a typical example of dolls made soon after the trademark registration, reveals no clue as to which member of the Société produced it.*

HT: 14in (35cm)

c.1910 S.F.B.J. DOLLY FACE GIRL (RIGHT)

Bisque socket head, marked on back and neck

Inset blue-gray glass eyes, with dark pupils

Brown mohair wig

The bisque socket head of this doll is incised on the back below the hairline "S.F.B.J./PARIS/60" and on the neck "2." The double figures indicate that the head was made from mold number 60 – a dolly face style that was a best-seller for the Société. The size, 2, corresponds to the height of the doll. Ht: 20in (50cm)

Black velvet dress

Composition arms, jointed at wrists, shoulders, and elbows

A. LANTERNIER GIRL (BELOW)

Founded in 1855, the A. Lanternier and Cie. porcelain factory in Limoges, France, made bisque dolls and heads from 1915 to 1924. The incised mark on this head bears the doll's name, Chérie. Other names on Lanternier heads are Favorite, La Georgienne, Toto, and Caprice. Ht: 27in (68cm)

Replacement human hair wig

Inset blue glass eyes

Bisque socket head, marked on back

Dress conceals composition body, jointed at shoulders, elbows, wrists, hips, and knees

J. VERLINGUE BISQUE SWIVEL HEAD (RIGHT)

Some companies did manage to survive outside the S.F.B.J. The small Parisian business of J. Verlingue traded between 1915 and the 1920s. This head of one of its lady dolls is teamed with a gusseted kid body. Ht: 15in (38cm)

Pierced ears

Highly tinted bisque swivel head and shoulder plate

Incised on the back of the head, below the hairline, the mark reads "PETITE FRANÇAISE/J V/FRANCE/1/LIANE." The company's anchor trademark can be seen between the J and V.

Chestnut brown mohair wig

Sleeping brown glass eyes; top lashes are made of animal hair

Dress conceals composition legs, jointed at hips and knees

Open mouth, with well-defined, molded top teeth

Swiss cotton pinafore

Composition arms, jointed at shoulders, elbows, and wrists

Hands are molded to show separate fingers and thumbs

MIGNON (RIGHT)

The trade name Mignon was used for dolls made by Felix Arena of Paris. It is coupled on this bisque socket head – made in Germany for Felix Arena – with the company's mark: a symbol resembling a biplane or box kite. The mark was registered in 1918 and was used for the following two years. Ht: 26in (65cm)

Doll's cotton print frock is not original, but is in period style

Dress hides composition legs and torso, jointed at knees and hips

Elaborately patterned knitted wool socks

Ankle-strap leather shoes, with ribbon bows

Leather-cloth boots, with leather soles, originally belonged to a small child

Leather shoes, with leather thong ties

German Marks of Distinction

· 1860s to 1920s ·

THURINGIA BECAME ESTABLISHED as Germany's most important porcelain-producing region from the start of the nineteenth century. Many firms whose main product was porcelain tableware manufactured bisque doll heads and sometimes limbs on behalf of German and French doll-makers that did not have their own porcelain factories, but bought and assembled doll parts, then sold the finished dolls under their own trade name. Simon and Halbig, established in 1869, was one of these manufacturers. Its production plant and facilities, located at Gräfenhain (near Ohrdruf in Thuringia) were very near the Alt, Beck and Gottschalck factory. Both firms produced many types of high-quality bisque doll heads. Among them were those molded and painted to show highly decorative hairstyles (see pages 44–51).

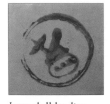

Jutta doll bodies were manufactured by Cuno and Otto Dressel. The firm's winged helmet mark is stamped in red ink on the doll's right shoulder.

Ears are pierced on the lobes

Curled blond mohair wig, with left-side parting

Molded and painted eyebrows

Bisque socket head, marked on back below hairline

Composition arms, jointed at elbows, shoulders, and wrists

Composition torso, molded as a child's body

Jointed knees; legs can bend backward, but not forward

Composition legs

Red paint defines toes and toe-nails

Sleeping violet-blue glass eyes, with top lashes of animal hair

Open mouth, with well-defined, molded top teeth

Base of fingernails is outlined with red paint

Joints at wrists allow hands to rotate

Ball joints at hips give legs forward, backward, and sideways movement

Doll wears lace-trimmed Swiss cotton dress over two cotton petticoats and baggy knickers

Expressively modeled hands have separate fingers and thumbs

SIMON AND HALBIG HEAD

The bisque socket head, marked with the mold number 1349, identifies this c.1910 doll. The number appears on the dolly face heads that were produced by Simon and Halbig for Cuno and Otto Dressel's Jutta dolls – a line made between 1906 and 1928.

HT: 22in (55cm)

Blond mohair wig

Inset blue glass eyes

Pierced ears

Orange-painted closed mouth

Pale bisque swivel head and shoulder plate

"ANNIE" (ABOVE) This head is incised "905," a mold number used by Simon and Halbig c. 1888 for a range of dolly face swivel heads on shoulder plates. Doll ht: 12in (30cm)

DOLLY FACE (BELOW) "S & H," marked on the back of this doll's bisque socket head, was Simon and Halbig's first trademark, registered in 1905. Ht: 19in (48cm)

Dark blond mohair wig

Inset blue paperweight glass eyes

Closed mouth

SIMON AND HALBIG LOOK-ALIKE (LEFT) Although the bisque socket head of this late 19th-century German doll closely resembles Simon and Halbig heads of the same period, its incised number, 93, does not correspond to any known Simon and Halbig mold. Ht: 23in (58cm)

Clothes conceal a composition body

DOLL MARKS

Many heads look similar, but study of the marks may point to different makers.

Simon and Halbig's Jutta heads bear the doll's name, mold number, size, and trademark.

Alt, Beck and Gottschalck used the number 698 for shoulder heads with cut-out pates.

Brown mohair wig

Sleeping blue glass eyes

Open mouth, with molded top teeth

Double chin and full cheeks are typical dolly face features

Wooden arms, jointed at wrists, elbows, and shoulders

Composition hands

Clothing hides composition torso and legs, jointed at hips and knees

Dress of a 1920s bride

Kid shoes and cotton socks

Curly blond mohair wig

Inset brown glass eyes

Heavily painted, feathered eyebrows

Bisque shoulder head is attached to a stuffed cloth body

POST-1880 ALT, BECK AND GOTTSCHALCK HEAD (ABOVE) The mark incised across the back lower edge of this shoulder head appears to be one used by Alt, Beck and Gottschalck (see Doll Marks, above right). The doll's face is modeled to show the chubby roundness and solemn expression of a young child. Doll ht: 13in (33cm)

SIMON AND HALBIG MOLD NUMBER 905 (RIGHT) Seen from a different angle, the pursed lips of the 905 dolly face are much more evident in this head than in that of "Annie" (see above left). Both dolls have gusseted kid bodies and bisque lower arms. Ht: 17in (43cm)

Straight blond mohair wig over a cork pate

Inset blue-gray glass eyes

Bisque swivel head

Stuffed kid arms, with gussets at elbows

Bisque hands, with short, fat fingers and indented knuckles

Outfit conceals a stuffed kid torso and legs

German Character Dolls

· 1880s to 1900s ·

WHILE MAKERS IN FRANCE continued to create dolls of an almost idealized femininity and beauty, German companies of the late nineteenth century turned their attention toward a novel idea: dolls with facial features modeled on those of real people. Although several manufacturers produced their own versions of these character dolls, as they were called, Kämmer and Reinhardt – founded in 1886 at Waltershausen in Thuringia by doll designer Ernst Kämmer and Franz Reinhardt, a salesman – was the first company to register Character Dolls as a trade name, in 1909.

Kämmer and Reinhardt made only doll bodies, but also produced complete dolls using bisque heads made to its specifications by one of the German porcelain factories. The heads for its character dolls were made by Simon and Halbig (see pages 68–69) and are said to have been modeled on the grandchildren of the company's two founding partners.

Bisque socket head, colored pink to represent a white baby

Molded, painted blond hair

Pale, delicately painted eyebrows

Intaglio eyes, painted pale blue with black pupils

Molded and painted dark brown hair

Intaglio eyes, painted brown

Heavily painted dark eyebrows

Baby mouth, with bowed top lip and droopy lower lip

Mouth is molded into an open smile

Robe conceals a bent-limb, flesh pink composition body, jointed at shoulders and hips

Bisque socket head, colored brown to represent a black baby

Deeply creased double chin

Second and third fingers are molded together; separate thumbs

Bent-limb composition body, jointed at shoulders and hips, painted brown to match coloring of the head

HT: 15in (38cm)

THE BABY *The first of the character dolls to be registered, the Baby head bears the mold number, 100, together with the marks of both Kämmer and Reinhardt and Simon and Halbig. The same mold was used to produce both white and black heads, despite the dissimilar facial characteristics of the ethnic groups that the two colors were intended to represent.*

Black mohair wig

Sleeping brown glass eyes

Open mouth, with molded top teeth

AFRICAN GIRL (LEFT) The Dolls of Four Races were made in Germany between 1890 and 1910, and included European, Oriental, and Indian dolls as well as this African girl. Its Simon and Halbig bisque socket head was a standard dolly face that was "transformed" with the aid of colored glazes, hair, and eyes. Ht: 17in (43cm)

Colored wood and composition body

Miniature, long-haired version of large doll is 5in (13cm) high

PETER (RIGHT) Heads designed to wear wigs were often given both a boy's and a girl's name. This bisque socket head is a Kämmer and Reinhardt mold number 101, registered in 1909 as Peter and Marie, and made by Simon and Halbig. It has Kämmer and Reinhardt's trademark and the mold number. Ht: 19in (48cm)

First used in 1895, the trademark shows an "&" within a six-point star, flanked by the initials "K" and "R."

Short blond mohair wig

Intaglio eyes, painted brown

Closed mouth

Composition arms, jointed at elbows, wrists, and shoulders

Composition torso, molded to show a child's rotund belly

Composition legs, jointed at knees and hips

Body is jointed at knees, hips, elbows, wrists, and shoulders

Feet are molded to show joined toes, defined with red paint lines

Flirty, sleeping glass eyes

Pierced ears

Bisque socket head, with mohair wig and inset blue glass eyes

Dress conceals composition body, jointed at shoulders and hips

Lower legs are molded and painted to show stockings and shoes

Human hair wig

Open mouth, showing four molded top teeth

Painted intaglio eyes

Incised on the nape of the doll's neck, the mold number, registered in 1909, appears directly below the Kämmer and Reinhardt trademark.

EUROPEAN GIRL (RIGHT)

Designed as one of the Dolls of Four Races (see African Girl above), this dolly face has a Simon and Halbig bisque socket head, and flesh pink, fully jointed composition body. A special attraction is its blue glass eyes, which move from side to side in a flirtatious way. Ht: 17in (43cm)

ELISE (ABOVE) Mold number 109, called Elise, is one of the rarest of all the Kämmer and Reinhardt character dolls. The head is modeled to show a child's face wearing a rather solemn expression. It has a long mohair wig, styled with a left-side parting and drawn into a bun behind, and intaglio eyes, painted blue-gray. The molded mouth is closed, but deeply indented between its full lips. Doll ht: 19in (48cm)

German Doll-makers

· 1890s to 1930s ·

BY THE END OF THE 1800S, many German factories were involved in the increasingly lucrative doll industry. Some produced only heads, others only bodies; some made the whole doll, and others bought the parts and simply assembled them. A number of these companies started small and expanded gradually. This growth enabled them to produce, assemble, and distribute dolls worldwide.

∿ One such company was Cuno and Otto Dressel of Sonneberg, in Thuringia. Its already established history of trading in dolls and toys had led, by this time, to a flourishing business producing composition doll parts, including heads. Bisque heads were made for the company by leading manufacturers of porcelain, such as Simon and Halbig (see pages 68–69) and Armand Marseille (see pages 76–79).

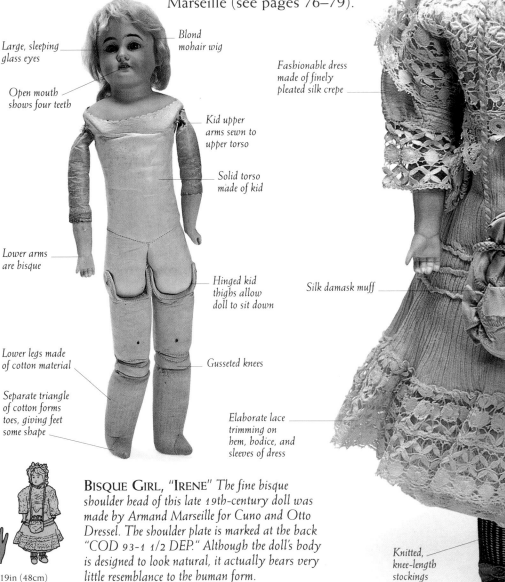

Large, sleeping glass eyes

Blond mohair wig

Open mouth shows four teeth

Kid upper arms sewn to upper torso

Solid torso made of kid

Lower arms are bisque

Hinged kid thighs allow doll to sit down

Lower legs made of cotton material

Gusseted knees

Separate triangle of cotton forms toes, giving feet some shape

Shoulder head is turned flatteringly to the side

Fashionable dress made of finely pleated silk crepe

Silk damask muff

Elaborate lace trimming on hem, bodice, and sleeves of dress

Knitted, knee-length stockings

Silk shoes with leather soles

BISQUE GIRL, "IRENE" The fine bisque shoulder head of this late 19th-century doll was made by Armand Marseille for Cuno and Otto Dressel. The shoulder plate is marked at the back "COD 93-1 1/2 DEP." Although the doll's body is designed to look natural, it actually bears very little resemblance to the human form.

HT: 19in (48cm)

Molded and painted hair

Blue intaglio eyes

Open/closed mouth

Composition body with bent limbs

Bisque socket head

The head mark probably dates from 1926.

J.D. KESTNER DOLLY FACE GIRL (RIGHT) Every company produced its own version of the Dolly Face doll, a universally popular line, along with other, less appealing designs. All these dolls, which could be dressed as girls or boys, have the rounded, slightly double-chinned face of a young child, an open mouth showing teeth, and inset or sleeping eyes. This example has unusual eyes that are brown with a black pupil. Ht: 18½in (47cm)

Doll is jointed only at hips and shoulders

BABY DOLL (ABOVE) The doll's face and mark resemble those of a Gebrüder Heubach character, but its head was made by Wiefel and Co. Operating from 1912 to the 1930s, this porcelain factory was taken over by Gustav Heubach and Robert Carl in 1926. Ht: 9in (23cm)

Dress conceals composition body, jointed at wrists, shoulders, elbows, hips, and knees

Blond mohair wig

Sleeping eyes are light blue glass

Open mouth has five teeth

C. AND O. DRESSEL LADY WITH ARMAND MARSEILLE HEAD (LEFT) These dolls were first made in 1893. The number 93 (see mark below) was registered by Armand Marseille with C.O.D. in 1892, and probably stands for 1893. A.M. shoulder heads are usually also marked "AM/Made in Germany." Ht: 14½in (37cm)

Sleeves conceal cloth upper arms and torso

Bisque lower arms

Beneath dress doll has composition legs, jointed at knees

The mark, incised on the side of the shoulder plate, clearly identifies this particular model.

Silk shoes stamped on leather soles "MADE IN GERMANY"

GEBRÜDER HEUBACH DOLLY FACE GIRL (LEFT) This c.1900 doll shows an example of a Dolly Face by another famous maker. With its bisque head and composition body, it looks quite similar to the Kestner version, but this model has sleeping blue glass eyes, and a tongue has been added to create a more realistic effect. Ht: 20in (50cm)

Bisque socket head with mohair wig

Sleeping eyes are operated by a lead weight

Stylish costume, made c.1920 from racing silks

Silk and lace parasol

Composition hands, jointed at wrists

"Lady Betty Modish"

· 1902 to 1911 ·

THE GERMAN COMPANY J.D. Kestner was founded in 1805 and operated throughout the nineteenth century into the 1930s from its premises in Waltershausen, Thuringia. Its first all-wooden dolls were followed by dolls with composition heads on cloth bodies. By the late 1890s, the company was manufacturing bisque doll heads from its factory in Ohrdruf. ∾ Cooperative trading agreements were common at this time, and many Kestner heads were sold to doll-making firms that did not produce heads of their own. Others were attached to Kestner composition bodies. Completed dolls were exported as far as the United States. Here, fortune smiled on one special doll, and in 1902, "Lady Betty Modish" entered the whirl of fashionable Boston society.

"Gold" metal hair-band, set with pearls and horsehair cockade

Blond human hair wig

Inset brown glass eyes, with finely painted lashes

Open mouth shows four top teeth

Pearl necklace matches the hair ornament

Composition hands, with separate fingers and thumbs

Shoulders are decorated with satin fabric rosebuds and curled ribbons

Evening gown, made of cream satin, with white net overskirt and low-cut bodice

Satin ribbons and appliquéd flowers, hand-stitched to overskirt

Long blond mohair wig

Bisque dolly face socket head

Wooden disks add strength to jointed parts

Inside body, elastic stringing holds the parts together

Composition torso, with defined waist and curvy hips

Composition arms, jointed at elbows and shoulders

Wooden balls at elbows allow arms to move

Composition hands, jointed at wrists

Composition upper legs, jointed at hips

Tops of legs are shaped so that legs can move freely

Rounded knees and thighs

Wooden balls at knees allow upper and lower legs to move to and fro

Flat feet; red paint detail on molded toes

HT: 18in (46cm)

MODEST MISS *The dressed doll at right cuts a fashionable figure, with its lady doll bisque socket head made from mold number 162 and its evening gown, designed and stitched by two Boston ladies. As the gown cannot be taken off, a similar Kestner doll shows the composition body that "Lady Betty Modish" is unable to reveal.*

VISITING OUTFIT (LEFT) *Lavish costumes for all occasions were created for "Lady Betty Modish," despite the doll's attachment to its evening gown. This sumptuous, richly colored ensemble is for winter wear.*

Satin blouse, with center panel of guipure lace

Purple velvet jacket; sleeves are lined for warmth

Cuffs and collar are trimmed with rabbit fur

Purple velvet-covered cocked hat, with ostrich-feather trim

Inset stiffened lace crown

Purple velvet skirt, made in six panels for extra fullness

Pleated cerise silk dust ruffle

DOLL MARKS
J.D. Kestner first registered mold numbers for its bisque shoulder and socket heads in 1897.

~

Incised marks often include "Made in Germany."

Kestner composition bodies have a red ink stamp mark on the torso or buttocks.

52 tiny playing cards: a complete pack

BOUDOIR ACCESSORIES (LEFT AND BELOW) *The miniature personal items that "Lady Betty Modish" takes into her "private apartments" are as elegant as any piece of the doll's stylish wardrobe. Still in pristine condition, they are an integral part of this unique collection.*

Nail buffer, with ivory back and chamois pad

Ivory nailbrush, with hair bristles

Dolly's Manicure

Manicure scissors

Metal nail file

Leather stationery wallet, with writing paper and envelopes

Metal bag frame, bound with crochet cotton

Silk damask knitting bag

Knitting in progress: a lacy bed jacket

RIDING HABIT (BELOW) *In the early 20th century, hunting was a very popular sport, but no lady would have considered sitting astride a horse. This costume is designed for riding sidesaddle, with a specially cut skirt that permits the merest glimpse of a leather booted leg.*

Cream silk stock, secured with a "gold" pin

Brown wool jacket, with nipped-in waist

Long-sleeved striped silk blouse

Wool skirt fastens at side with four fabric-covered buttons

Loop at top

Knitted woolen riding hose

Cotton spats, worn over boots

Pearl button fastening

Buckled straps go under the feet to keep the spats in place

Black and tan leather riding boots, with metal buckles

Armand Marseille Dolls

· 1890s to 1930s ·

BORN IN THE RUSSIAN CITY of St. Petersburg in 1856, Armand Marseille later emigrated with his family to Thuringia in Germany. The region supported a well-established toy- and doll-making industry, which soon captured the young man's interest. In 1885, he bought the porcelain factory of Liebermann and Wegescher in Köppelsdorf and began to manufacture bisque doll heads there five years later. The business went from triumph to triumph. Armand Marseille became one of the largest German manufacturers of bisque doll heads.

Most of the heads made from 1890 to 1920 are the socket type, well cast and finished. The open-mouth, smiling dolly face head of mold number 390 was the most popular. Later heads show a marked deterioration in the quality of the company's workmanship.

Short brown mohair wig, styled in a bowl haircut

Inset dark blue-gray glass eyes

Wig is secured to the head with glue

Bisque socket head, incised "Armand Marseille/Germany/996/A.6.M."

Inside torso, arms are strung with elastic from left to right shoulder

Bent arms, made of composition

Hip joints allow doll to sit down

Inside torso, legs are strung to head with elastic

Square feet are flat, with no instep

Mouth is molded to show a separate tongue and two top teeth

Composition torso, modeled to show a child's rounded belly and chest

Straight, unjointed composition legs, with chubby knees

Indistinctly defined toes

Enameled golliwog, pinned to wool dickey

White silk facings and a collar edged with crocheted cotton

Full sleeves, gathered into narrow cuffs

Hands have separate thumbs and fingers

Hip-length belt, a popular fashion of the 1920s

Long, fine wool coat, with front button fastening

Wool trousers match the coat

White cotton socks

White kid shoes, tied with purple-red satin ribbon

LATE 1920S BOY *The mold number, 996, incised on the nape of this doll's neck, appears in the records of Armand Marseille as a baby socket head, with inset or sleeping glass eyes, a molded open/closed mouth, and a wig. Unlike most baby dolls, which feature molded, unjointed bent limbs, this example has straight legs that allow it to stand without support on its flat feet.*

HT: 19in (48cm)

Mohair wig

Bisque socket head, incised "1894/AM 4/ oX DI"

Closed, pursed-lip mouth

"Germany/ 996/A.3.M." is incised on head

Bisque socket head

DOLL MARKS

Heads are usually incised at the back, below the hairline or on the neck.

The mold number and head size appear below the maker's name and country.

TYROLEAN BOY

(ABOVE) *This late 1930s socket head is typical of those produced by Armand Marseille after its boom years. Although the coloring of the head and facial features is quite well done, the finish is rather harsh and considerably less refined than that of earlier heads. Doll ht: 17in (43cm)*

Outfit covers a composition and wood body, jointed at the knees, hips, elbows, and shoulders

Clothes hide composition torso, jointed at hips and shoulders, with straight legs and bent arms

DOLLY FACE GIRL (LEFT) *In the 1930s, this type of doll, with a pretty face and robust, partly jointed composition body, was considered to be an ideal and inexpensive play doll for young children. Ht: 16in (40cm)*

Mohair wig

Molded eyebrows

Sleeping blue glass eyes

Mohair wig

EARLY 1900S BOY CRICKETER (ABOVE)
Wholesale dolls were often exported and sold unclothed. This dolly face boy's classic cricketing attire – wool shirt and flannels, with a striped blazer and cap – was made by a mother, based on her son's own sporting togs. A tin-box cricket bat completes the outfit. Ht: 14in (35cm)

Open mouth has four molded top teeth

Inset blue glass eyes

Open mouth shows four teeth

FLORODORA (RIGHT) *The trade name Florodora was registered in 1901 for mold number 1374, a bisque socket head. Produced until 1921, many heads were exported to the United States for George Borgfeldt's My Playmate line of dolls. Ht: 16in (40cm)*

c.1900 RED CROSS NURSE (RIGHT) *The familiar dolly face socket head of Armand Marseille mold number 390 is teamed in this doll with an unmarked composition body. Many bodies are so similar in style that it is almost impossible to identify their individual makers if they have no marks. Ht: 16in (40cm)*

Dress conceals fully jointed composition body

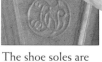

The shoe soles are stamped with two German script letters.

~ My Dream Baby ~

· 1920s to 1930s ·

UNTIL THE START of the nineteenth century, the word "baby" was used for all dolls, including those representing older children or adults. The very few dolls that were designed to portray babies had neither the facial features nor the body type of their human counterparts, but were simply made shorter than "older" dolls. By 1850, some manufacturers in France and Germany had registered *Bébé* and Baby as trade names, but the dolls so named still resembled young children rather than babies.

~ In 1909, Kämmer and Reinhardt registered its first character doll baby head (see pages 70–71), along with a special design of bent-limb composition body, and baby dolls began to look like babies. Armand Marseille's mid-1920s version was issued in Germany as My Dream Baby. Heads were sold to other doll producers, including the Averill Manufacturing Co. of New York, which used them for its Lullaby Baby doll line.

Spray-painted, muted color suggests downy hair covering

Softly painted eyebrows

Sleeping blue-gray glass eyes, without lashes

Small, tightly closed mouth

Deep, low forehead

Small eyes are set wide apart

Squat, button nose, with flat bridge

Chubby hands, with separate thumbs and partly joined fingers

Lace trim at sleeve and neck edges

Bisque socket head, marked on back "Germany/341/ 4.K/A.M."

Composition arms, with bent elbows

Inside torso, arms are jointed at shoulders with elastic stringing

Red paint lines define joined parts of fingers

V-shaped red paint lines between thumbs and first fingers

Composition torso, modeled as a rounded baby body

Inside torso, legs are jointed at hips with elastic stringing

Cream silk baby robe

Composition legs, molded to show dimpled bent knees

Deep creases between legs and feet

Slightly upturned, stubby feet

MOLD NUMBER 341 *Armand Marseille produced more than one style of My Dream Baby. This doll shows the better-quality type. It has a bisque socket head with closed mouth and a bent-limb composition body, designed so that the doll can sit with splayed legs, but not stand.*

HT: 16in (40cm)

Bisque socket head, marked on back "A. M./ Germany/ 351/3.K"

Painted hair, with small curls molded on forehead

Puffy, swollen eye sockets, typical of a newborn baby

Open mouth has two molded bottom teeth

Painted hair; no molded detail

Fine brush-strokes indicate eyelashes

Sleeping pale blue-gray glass eyes

Composition body with bent limbs

DOLL MARKS

Mold number 341 identifies a bisque socket head with closed mouth.

Mold number 351 identifies a bisque socket head with open mouth. "K" for Kurbelkopf indicates a socket head.

CLOSED-MOUTH SOCKET HEAD (ABOVE) Although every head was cast from mold number 341 or 351, the hand-painting of the features makes each one look slightly different. This example, marked "A. M./Germany/341/ 0.K," has the characteristic My Dream Baby face, but with top and bottom lashes painted around the eyes. Doll ht: 12in (30cm)

MOLD NUMBER 351 (ABOVE) Another version of the My Dream Baby bisque socket head, this example shows an open mouth with molded bottom teeth, a design that seems at odds with the concept of a newborn infant. Ht: 12in (30cm)

BLACK BABY (RIGHT) Three other colors of head were issued in addition to the white ones representing Caucasian babies. Described in the words that were used in the 1920s, they are: brown, for "mulatto"; cream, for "Oriental"; and black, for "Negro," shown here. Ht: 24in (60cm)

Molded and painted black hair

Inset very dark brown glass eyes

White bisque socket head, colored brown

Closed-mouth white bisque socket head, colored cream

Original ikat-patterned silk kimono

Inset black glass eyes, with painted lashes

Darker crossline accentuates fullness of lips

Hands, shaped as fists, have separate thumbs

Wooden baby rattle, hand-carved in India

Dress conceals slightly bent legs of colored composition, jointed at the hips

Curved arms, jointed at shoulders, made of colored composition

Costume hides a composition body, colored cream

Broad feet, with poorly defined molded toes

ORIENTAL BABY (ABOVE) Like the black baby, the Oriental head was cast from one of the standard molds used for "white" dolls, with no attempt made at modeling ethnic features. The finger and toe lines, painted orange instead of red, are a special feature. Ht: 9in (23cm)

Bisque Baby Dolls
· 1900s to 1990s ·

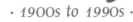

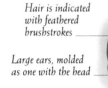

THE POPULARITY OF BISQUE-HEADED baby dolls peaked during the 1920s, with the introduction of named models such as George Borgfeldt's Bye-Lo Baby in the United States and Armand Marseille's My Dream Baby in Germany. Many were the product of German manufacturers, whose skilled modeling of character heads satisfied the increasing demand for dolls with realistic features. Designed as newborn infants or older babies, the dolls have heads showing their makers' styles, attached to a common body type.

A typical 1920s baby doll has a bisque socket head – most often with molded and painted hair – and a plump composition body. Its unjointed, curved limbs are strung with elastic at the shoulders, so that the arms can move, and at the hips, to allow the doll to sit.

Head is modeled to show the features of a newborn baby

Inset blue glass eyes

Molded top teeth

Hair is indicated with feathered brushstrokes

Painted eyebrows

Large ears, molded as one with the head

Human hair lashes, glued into inside top edges of eye sockets

Chin, mouth, and nose are modeled to show deep creases

Open mouth; tongue is molded with bottom lip

Jointed shoulders allow arms to move to and fro

Chubby, curved arms; no elbow joints

Hands have separate thumbs; second and third fingers are molded together

Creases at waist suggest fleshy folds

Composition torso, with rotund belly and rounded chest

Jointed hips allow doll to sit with wide-apart legs

Chubby, curved legs; no knee joints

Traditional christening robe, made of white cotton lawn

Front of robe is edged all around with a border of broderie anglaise

Robe hides period baby undergarments: white cotton undershirt and diaper; cream wool long crossover bodice; and white, lace-trimmed cotton petticoat

Feet are modeled to show flexed toes, a typical baby movement

MODEL BABY *The finely cast and detailed bisque socket head of this early 20th-century doll is incised "151," a mold number that was registered by several companies, including Hertel, Schwab and Co., to which the head is attributed. The composition body, also of high quality, is a superb example of the bent-limb style that was specially designed for baby dolls.*

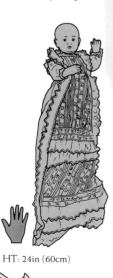

HT: 24in (60cm)

NEWBORN INFANT (LEFT) This character baby was made by Willy Weyh of Sonneberg in Germany in 1925. It has a bisque flange neck head with a stuffed cloth torso, arms, and legs, and molded composition hands, cast to the wrist joints.
Ht: 12in (30cm)

Painted eyelashes

Inset blue glass eyes

Small closed mouth

The size of the head, 2, appears below the name of the maker as part of the mark.

Brown human hair wig

Metal eyelids, with hair lashes

Sleeping blue glass eyes

Bisque socket head

The mark incised below the hairline on the back of the head shows the maker's initials and the mold number.

Second and third fingers are joined together, except at tips

Composition bent limbs

Clothes hide composition body, jointed at hips and shoulders

ADVANCED BABY (ABOVE)
Forsaking realism, some makers used wigs to soften the bald heads of their baby dolls, particularly those that were made to portray older children. This c.1916 example is the work of J.D. Kestner. Ht: 18in (46cm)

Hair is lightly painted in parallel lines

Fine brown paint lines define upper rims of eye sockets

Molded and painted eyes

At back of head, maker's mark reads "FB/0"

Open/closed mouth

c.1911 CHARACTER BABY
(LEFT) Inspired by Kämmer and Reinhardt's first character doll, Baby (see page 70), this model has a bisque socket head made by the German company Fritz Bierschenk. Its bent-limb body is designed as that of a healthy young baby.
Ht: 11in (28cm)

Curves of eye sockets are defined with brown paint lines

Painted light blue eyes

Closed mouth, modeled with very full lips

Hand-painted mark below left ear: "LER 92/Tilly/160"

Double chin, a baby doll feature

1992 BABY GIRL, TILLY
(ABOVE) A traditionally styled doll that brings bisque up to date, Tilly was handcrafted by English doll artists Lynne and Michael Roche. The doll has a bisque flange neck head, with spray-painted hair. Its bent lower arms and legs are also bisque, while the upper limbs and rounded torso are made of firmly stuffed cloth. Ht: 8in (20cm)

Curved bisque legs, cast to above knee joints

Dress conceals a composition body, jointed at hips and shoulders

Lesser-known German Makers

· 1900s to 1930s ·

AS THE HUB OF THE GERMAN porcelain industry, Thuringia supported numerous small doll-makers as well as the factories that manufactured doll heads for large companies. The work of these lesser-known makers has often survived not because the dolls are of superior quality, but simply because they were made in great numbers. Considered playthings to be thrown away when broken, very large quantities were produced. Even the businesses of smaller makers were sustained by the public demand for such dolls.

These two pages show the work of less celebrated German makers. Each doll has a bisque head incised with the marks of a known and recognized manufacturer. Finding identifiable marks is a stroke of luck, as many makers did not mark their products.

Titian mohair or human hair wig

Painted top and bottom eyelashes

Sleeping blue glass eyes

Ears are pierced for earrings

Sleeping eyes, with metal lids, in half-closed position

Open mouth, showing four top teeth

Simon and Halbig bisque socket head, marked on back "79/10/Germany/ HANDWERCK"

Separate thumbs and spread fingers

Composition arms, jointed at elbows, shoulders, and wrists

Composition torso, molded to show a child's pronounced belly and small chest

Arms are painted flesh pink

Cotton lawn dress, trimmed with satin ribbon, lace, and broderie anglaise

Composition upper legs, shaped at tops of thighs so doll can sit easily

Wooden balls give upper and lower legs easy movement

Composition lower legs, with curved calves

Red paint lines define finger- nail ridges

Painted red toe and toenail detail

Chubby, creased ankles

HEINRICH HANDWERCK

Founded in 1855 as a toy-making company, Heinrich Handwerck later switched to composition doll bodies, which were attached to Handwerck-designed Simon and Halbig bisque heads. This finely modeled c.1900 dolly face girl typifies one of the most popular styles of the period.

Color coordinated cotton socks

Pigskin shoes, with metal buckles

HT: 19in (48cm)

Blond
mohair wig

Inset brown
glass eyes

Bisque
socket head

Open mouth, with
four top teeth

The mark, incised on
the back of the head,
also includes "Germany/
4" below the designer-
maker's name. Max
Handwerck operated
in Waltershausen from
1900 until the 1930s.

The Hermann
Steiner mark
shows an "H"
entwined with
"St."; size number
is below.

Composition body, jointed
at shoulders, elbows,
wrists, hips, and knees

Hands jointed
at wrists

MAX HANDWERCK, GIRL
(ABOVE) *The composition doll bodies
made by this company were teamed
with one of two types of bisque head,
many of which were produced in the
porcelain factory of William Goebel.
Socket heads, like this one, came with
sleeping glass eyes and mohair wigs.
Shoulder heads were usually finished
with molded and painted hair and
painted eyes. Doll ht: 27in (68cm)*

HERMANN STEINER, DOLLY
FACE (RIGHT) *In 1920, bisque doll
heads joined the stuffed plush animals
that had been Hermann Steiner's stock-
in-trade since the establishment of the
company in Neustadt in 1911. This
example, made in the 1920s, has a
composition torso and fully jointed
wooden limbs. Steiner still produces
toys but not dolls. Ht: 17in (43cm)*

Blond mohair wig, on
a bisque socket head

Sleeping blue glass
eyes, with hair lashes

C.1925 GIRL (RIGHT)
*Arthur Schoenau and Carl
Hoffmeister had already proved
their ability as doll-makers when
they joined forces in 1901 to form
the Schoenau and Hoffmeister
Porzellanfabrik Burggrub.
The company produced
its bisque doll heads —
of which this is a good
example — in its own
porcelain factory.
Ht: 28in (70cm)*

Dress hides a fully
jointed composition
torso and limbs

The incised mark
shows the initials
of the factory name
above the size
and mold
numbers.

Boots hide wooden legs,
with very long thighs,
jointed at knees and hips

Reddish brown
coarse mohair wig

Sleeping googly
blue glass eyes

Bisque socket head

Bisque arms,
jointed at
shoulders

J. WALTHER AND SOHN,
C.1920 GOOGLY-EYED
DOLL (RIGHT) *The charming
bisque character head of this
doll was made in the Oeslau,
Coburg, porcelain factory of
Johann Walther. It is incised
on the back with the crown
symbol of the firm, together
with "W & S" entwined.
Ht: 7in (18cm)*

Dress hides composition
legs and torso; lower legs
have molded and
painted shoes
and stockings

Ethnic and English Dolls

· 1860s to 1920s ·

THE STORY OF DOLLS and their makers has linked numerous countries not only through mutually beneficial trade and enterprise, but also as a result of historical events. Some of the most interesting and unusual dolls have been made during periods of conflict, or as designers tried to create new and exciting models that would spark the imagination of the buying public and – in so doing – loosen its purse strings. For many collectors, dolls of this kind have a very special charm that balances their sometimes idiosyncratic appearance. ∾ All the dolls described on these two pages illustrate how English and German manufacturers reacted to changes in their familiar worlds during the second half of the nineteenth century and the first two decades of the twentieth century – changes that led, on one hand, to broadened horizons and, on the other, to newly entrenched and insular attitudes.

Slanted, curved eyebrows: the only "realistic" facial feature

Closed mouth

Silk-covered cardboard hat has a braided silk trim

Pierced ears: a common feature of late 19th-century German doll heads

Tinted bisque socket head

Elbow-length sleeves are lined with pink silk

Incised under hair, "220": the mold number for an Oriental head, registered in 1888

Mohair wig, braided into a long pigtail

Hands have separate thumbs and joined fingers

Composition arms, jointed at shoulders

Front of silk jacket has faded from its original olive green color to dun brown

Back of jacket shows its original olive green color

Woven silk damask underskirt

Pink wool is braided in with the pigtail and secures its end

Small feet evoke the Chinese custom of foot-binding

Clothes hide composition legs, jointed at knees and hips and strung to a composition torso

Linen hose, with woven patterning

Split-sided tunic coat, made of dark blue silk

Pink silk also lines the body of the coat

Composition lower legs, molded and painted to show Chinese-style slippers and socks

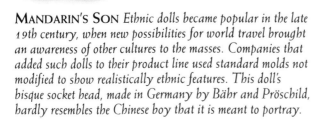

MANDARIN'S SON *Ethnic dolls became popular in the late 19th century, when new possibilities for world travel brought an awareness of other cultures to the masses. Companies that added such dolls to their product line used standard molds not modified to show realistically ethnic features. This doll's bisque socket head, made in Germany by Bähr and Pröschild, hardly resembles the Chinese boy that it is meant to portray.*

HT: 12in (30cm)

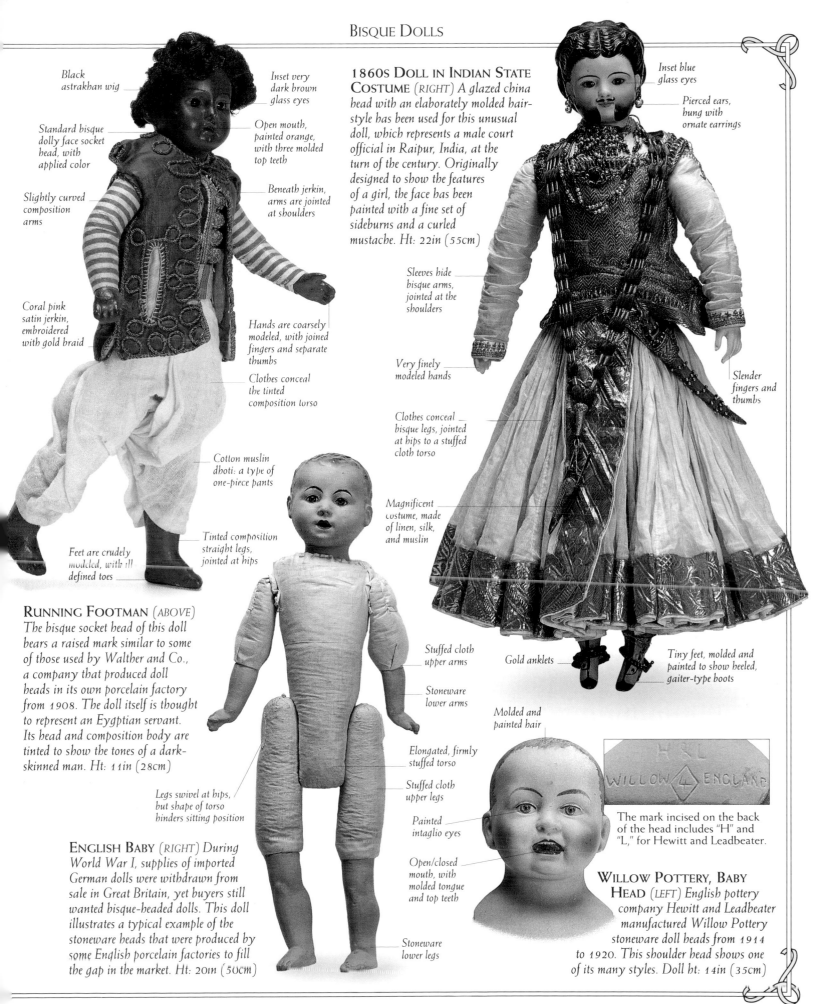

Black astrakhan wig

Standard bisque dolly face socket head, with applied color

Slightly curved composition arms

Coral pink satin jerkin, embroidered with gold braid

Inset very dark brown glass eyes

Open mouth, painted orange, with three molded top teeth

Beneath jerkin, arms are jointed at shoulders

Hands are coarsely modeled, with joined fingers and separate thumbs

Clothes conceal the tinted composition torso

Cotton muslin dhoti: a type of one-piece pants

Feet are crudely modeled, with ill-defined toes

1860s DOLL IN INDIAN STATE COSTUME (RIGHT)
A glazed china head with an elaborately molded hairstyle has been used for this unusual doll, which represents a male court official in Raipur, India, at the turn of the century. Originally designed to show the features of a girl, the face has been painted with a fine set of sideburns and a curled mustache. Ht: 22in (55cm)

Inset blue glass eyes

Pierced ears, hung with ornate earrings

Sleeves hide bisque arms, jointed at the shoulders

Very finely modeled hands

Clothes conceal bisque legs, jointed at hips to a stuffed cloth torso

Magnificent costume, made of linen, silk, and muslin

Slender fingers and thumbs

Gold anklets

Tiny feet, molded and painted to show heeled, gaiter-type boots

RUNNING FOOTMAN (ABOVE)
The bisque socket head of this doll bears a raised mark similar to some of those used by Walther and Co., a company that produced doll heads in its own porcelain factory from 1908. The doll itself is thought to represent an Eygptian servant. Its head and composition body are tinted to show the tones of a dark-skinned man. Ht: 11in (28cm)

Stuffed cloth upper arms

Stoneware lower arms

Legs swivel at hips, but shape of torso hinders sitting position

Elongated, firmly stuffed torso

Stuffed cloth upper legs

Painted intaglio eyes

Stoneware lower legs

ENGLISH BABY (RIGHT)
During World War I, supplies of imported German dolls were withdrawn from sale in Great Britain, yet buyers still wanted bisque-headed dolls. This doll illustrates a typical example of the stoneware heads that were produced by some English porcelain factories to fill the gap in the market. Ht: 20in (50cm)

Molded and painted hair

Open/closed mouth, with molded tongue and top teeth

The mark incised on the back of the head includes "H" and "L," for Hewitt and Leadbeater.

WILLOW POTTERY, BABY HEAD (LEFT)
English pottery company Hewitt and Leadbeater manufactured Willow Pottery stoneware doll heads from 1914 to 1920. This shoulder head shows one of its many styles. Doll ht: 14in (35cm)

Mass-produced Bisque Dolls

· 1900s to 1940s ·

IN THE LATE NINETEENTH and early twentieth centuries, France and Germany cornered the market for bisque dolls. The glazed china and untinted bisque heads with elaborately molded hairstyles, prim-faced lady dolls in gorgeous attire, and character dolls of this period are some of the finest examples of doll-making. But after 1900, and particularly between World Wars I and II, new possibilities for world trade opened up, and encouraged the mass production of inexpensive dolls, as forward-looking manufacturers capitalized on an increasingly lucrative export market.

⌒ Such dolls are often of the "cheap and cheerful" variety. Many were produced to be sold at fairs and in amusement parks, or as vacation souvenirs; some were made as ornamental pieces, aimed more toward adult than child buyers, and can hardly be thought of as play dolls; others originated as fictional characters.

The designer's surname appears as a signature, impressed into the base of both feet.

Long wisps of hair, painted from knob on crown to forehead

Top of head is molded and painted to show a knob of hair

Large eyes, painted in the typically side-glancing position

Single molded and painted knob of hair on either side of head

Hair is painted in wispy brushstrokes at nape of neck

Molded, tiny button nose

Tiny molded wings, painted blue, a special Kewpie feature

Mouth is a single molded and painted line, set in a broad smile

Shoulder joints have metal pins that allow arms to move

Printed paper label shows the Kewpie trade name, registered by George Borgfeldt in 1913, and the doll's country of origin

All-bisque arms

All-bisque body, molded as one with the head

"Starfish" hands are typically upturned

Hands are molded to show separate thumbs and spread, slightly "webbed," fingers

Molded belly button, tinted with rosy pink highlights

Molded legs are joined together

Diminutive rump; paintwork accentuates each tiny buttock

Tinges of darker color define "hipline" at base of torso

Short, stubby feet

Depressions between ankles and thighs give shape to backs of legs

Legs are modeled to show a young child's chubby thighs

Splotches of color suggest knees

ALL-BISQUE KEWPIE *Based on the illustrations of Rose O'Neill in the* Ladies' Home Journal, *the original Kewpies were modeled by Joseph Kallus and produced by George Borgfeldt, a company in New York where Kallus worked as a designer. This doll is one of the earliest models, which were made in the porcelain factory of German doll manufacturer J.D. Kestner.*

Narrow grooves give definition to the molded, joined toes

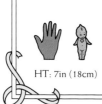

HT: 7in (18cm)

Molded and painted hair

Coarsely modeled facial features

Bisque shoulder head

Dumpy bisque lower arms

Well-modeled hair

Stuffed cloth upper arms

Bisque lower legs

Stuffed cloth upper legs and torso

Jester's hat is molded as part of the head

Arms are pinned to shoulders with bent-ended wires

Plump cheeks, painted to show a florid complexion

Paint highlights costume details

Lower arms are molded as gauntlets

Hips are strung with elastic

Lower legs are molded to show wide trouser hems

Bisque lower legs, painted to show shoes

Stiffened canvas hat, with braid trim and wool flowers

Mohair wig

Painted facial features

Ceramic arms, jointed at shoulders

Ceramic legs, jointed at hips

Lower legs are painted to show boots

JAPANESE DOLLS (ABOVE)

When Germany suspended the production of bisque dolls during World War I, the United States turned to Japan for supplies. This pair shows the poor quality of Japanese dolls made for export. Ht: Boy 7in (18cm); girl 6in (15cm)

RECLINING LADIES (RIGHT)

High-quality bisque figurines were popular ornaments between 1900 and 1930, their willowy, nude – or seminude – bodies gracing many a boudoir dressing table or mantel-piece. These two naturists, made in Germany c.1920, are unusually adorned with mohair wigs. Ht: 5in (13cm)

1920S CARNIVAL KEEPSAKE

(ABOVE) Made in Germany, this all-bisque figure has a one-piece head and torso, molded and painted to show a jester's costume. Crude joints at the shoulders and hips allow the limbs to swing when the doll is jiggled. Ht: 2½in (6cm)

1930S HOLIDAY

SOUVENIR (RIGHT) Though wearing the regional costume of Alsace in France, this doll is probably of German origin. Its head and torso, cast as a single unit, and unjointed limbs are all made of a low-grade ceramic material. Ht: 4in (10cm)

Gracefully angled head

Strawberry blond mohair wig; molded hair is more typical

Eyes and brows are delicately painted

Body is modeled to show a slim, curvy torso and slender limbs

Recumbent figures are the most often seen type

Body is fixed into an alluring "come-hither" position

Molded and painted hair

Well-modeled eyes, nose, and open/closed mouth

Wired joints at shoulders

Legs are jointed to one-piece torso and head with elastic stringing

1930S GERMAN BISQUE

BABIES (ABOVE) Inexpensively made in large numbers, small bisque dolls like these found a ready market among children as dolls' house figures. Many came fully clothed in pastel-colored crocheted garments. Ht: Largest 3in (7.5cm); smallest 1½in (4cm)

Feet are molded and painted to show slippers

Rag Dolls

Doll manufacturers in England and the United States introduced the first commercially made rag dolls in the 1850s. Soft, safe, and warm to cuddle, a rag doll was often a child's first toy. These were generally less sophisticated than dolls made from other materials, such as bisque or wood, but had great charm nonetheless. Unfortunately, rag dolls are not very hard-wearing; as a result, fewer survive than any other type of doll.

THERE IS OCCASIONALLY some confusion regarding the definitions of rag and cloth dolls. "Rag" is the general term used for dolls that are made of any fabric; this could be cotton, silk, velvet, felt, or any other suitable material. "Cloth," however, is a more specific term, used only to describe dolls made of linen or cotton, including calico (a coarse, plain, usually unbleached cotton) and muslin (a fine, plain-weave cotton fabric). Traditionally, rag dolls are stuffed with cloth, sawdust, straw, or kapok, which is a type of cotton. Since the 1950s, foam, foam chips, and even old nylon stockings have also been used.

well as the availability of the materials. However, any type of fabric could be used, and many a doll was made from an old rag or woolen remnants that could be found in the home.

Factory-made Rag Dolls

From the 1850s onward, rag dolls began to be produced commercially by English and American doll-makers. Designs were printed in color on flat sheets of fabric and were subsequently cut out, stitched, and stuffed. Sometimes only a flat representation of the front and back of the doll were shown; occasionally additional features and gussets were sewn on to make the body appear more lifelike and to give it a three-dimensional quality.

 Alternatively, the dolls' features could be painted rather than printed. This was a common practice, particularly in

Rag Doll Origins

For centuries, rag dolls were made at home by mothers as playthings for their children. Naturally, the quality and design of these homemade dolls tended to vary greatly, depending on the skill and imagination of the maker, as

GRANDMA COLE (*LEFT*)
This doll, representing a grandmother, is one of the members of the Cole Family (see page 93), created c.1901. It is thought that the doll may be a portrait of the doll-maker Roxanna Elizabeth McGee Cole, who was a resident of Conway, Arkansas. Ht: 22in (55cm)

"SOLID COMFORT"
(*RIGHT*) *The famous American doll-maker Izannah F. Walker produced this doll in 1873. It is made entirely from cloth. The facial features, hair curls, and black boots were delicately painted on by hand in oil colors. It is clothed in a printed, lace-trimmed cotton dress over plain cotton undergarments. Ht: 18in (43cm)*

FACE MASKS *(ABOVE) These 1920s masks, made of cotton stretched over a molded buckram base, were attached to prepared cloth heads and stockinette bodies. Ht: 6in (16cm) and 5½in (14cm)*

MAGAZINE ILLUSTRATION *(RIGHT) Published in* The Graphic *in 1879, "Rich girl, poor girl, both fond of dolls" illustrates how young girls, regardless of their social status, are fascinated by dolls.*

the United States. The doll would be put together, and then the facial features and hair were painted on. This was done by hand using oil colors. Occasionally the features were stitched on, or they could be painted on and then stitched. Human hair or mohair could be sewn onto the head or was made into wigs that were glued or stitched in place for a more realistic effect.

Rag Dolls in the Twentieth Century

By the twentieth century, manufacturing methods had greatly improved, and it was possible to emulate the more sophisticated jointed dolls made of materials such as bisque and composition. Many companies, such as Steiff (see pages 96–97) and Lenci (see pages 100–101) began to use felt for the heads, rather than cloth, for a more lifelike result. When treated with stiffening, felt can be pressed over a mold to give a doll raised features. The material, stiff enough to hold glass eyes or a wig, is easily painted. Sometimes doll bodies, as well as heads, were made of felt.

⌒ Doll-makers also began to use a knitted silk or cotton fabric called stockinette. Because of the soft, stretchy quality of the material, it is generally used for bodies rather than heads. However, if stretched over a molded, hollow, buckram (stiffened cloth) base, it is sufficiently rigid and can be painted. During the 1920s and 1930s, manufacturers produced a range of dolls with long, lean, stockinette bodies, styled on the fashionable body shape of the time. These soft bodies were attached to rigid, painted face masks (see above).

⌒ Velvet is also occasionally used in doll-making, but rarely for heads. However, the English doll manufacturer Norah Wellings (see pages 102–103) produced a considerable number of heads made of velvet. These were used particularly in the production

of her ethnic dolls. Velveteen, a cotton fabric with a short, thick pile, was sometimes used as a substitute for velvet in the manufacture of lower-quality dolls.

⌒ Today, rag dolls are still popular. They are made of modern, washable materials and, if health and safety guidelines are followed, are easily maintained. A few of the old manufacturers still survive, and continue to make rag dolls in the traditional ways.

RAGGEDY ANN *(RIGHT) Raggedy Ann began life as a cartoon illustration, created by American artist Johnny Gruelle. In 1915, he registered a trademark for the name "Raggedy Ann" and a logo, and began making and selling hand-crafted Raggedy Ann dolls. A candy heart with the words "I love you" was put in the chest of each doll. This model was made in China by Playskool, Inc., a subsidiary of Hasbro, Inc., in 1987. Ht: 12in (30cm)*

American Home Industry

· 1890s to 1930s ·

LIKE THE WOODEN DOLLS of the nineteenth century (see pages 14–15), American cloth dolls of this period have a charm that transcends their rather stolid appearance. Many designs started as playthings, made by mothers for their children. As the dolls became popular and treasured items among family and friends, the maker was urged to increase output, and the dolls went into small studio or factory production. These two pages show examples of work by such makers.

~ Emma E. Adams of Oswego, New York, began making dolls in the 1890s. In 1893, at the Chicago World's Fair, the Columbian Exposition Commission gave one of her dolls a "Diploma of Honorable Mention," and named it the Columbian Doll: "Columbia" is the female personification of the United States. Among the very first American patriotic dolls, the Columbians were produced until 1910.

1893 Columbian Exposition ribbon, from Miss Columbia's scrapbook journal.

Curly blond hair, painted in oil colors

Flat, painted features

Oil color continues from head down to top of chest

Lower arms are stiffened with small wooden stick inside

Lower arms are painted in flesh-toned oil colors

Stuffed muslin body, shaped to define waist

Seams at tops of thighs and knees allow limited movement

Original buttoned shoes and socks

Banner ribbon in traditional patriotic colors, with commemorative enameled pin

Cotton dress and undergarments are all handmade

CHILDREN'S CHARITY ENVOY *Miss Columbia is perhaps the most famous of the Columbian dolls. Made in 1899, and given by Adams to a wealthy Bostonian, Elizabeth Richards Horton, for her International Doll Collection, it toured the world raising money for charities, especially those benefiting children.*

HT: 19in (48cm)

Bisque sailor doll, German c.1900

Peg wooden, from Queen Alexandra and Edward VII

GIFTS AND SOUVENIRS (LEFT)
During its three-year journey, the Miss Columbia doll received a great many tokens, given for good luck, or as cheery remembrances of people seen and places visited.

Wooden water bottle

Fish pincushion, from Japan

Mohave Indian clay pipe

Cloth doll, from the Philippines

HOSPITAL DOLLS (RIGHT)
Martha Jenks Chase, a doctor's wife in Pawtucket, Rhode Island, developed the Hospital Dolls in 1910. Life-size and realistic, these baby and adult figures were used widely in hospital training, hence their name. The stockinette head is stretched over a mask molded to show facial details. Stitched seams provide jointing for the body. The entire doll is oil-painted. Ht: 24in (60cm)

Thumb is applied separately from fingers and hand

Stitched mark of St. Thomas's Hospital in London

Woolly hair is made of lint

MISS COLUMBIA'S CONSORT (LEFT)
This Uncle Sam doll, made in 1901 by Mrs. Covey of Los Angeles, California, traveled with the Miss Columbia doll as its male counterpart and "companion," also representing the United States. Its cloth body is unjointed, and its head and hands are oil-painted. Ht: 20in (50cm)

Painted blond hair on forehead and around edges of face

ALABAMA INDESTRUCTIBLES
(RIGHT) Designed by Ella Louise Gauntt Smith of Roanoke, Alabama, these handmade dolls were factory-produced for the Ella Smith Doll Co. from 1900 to 1925. The ears are a distinctive feature. Ht: 14½in (37cm)

Round cloth pate at top of head

Applied ears

Human hair wig

Stiffened, molded cloth head

Flange neck allows head to turn

Oil paint covers the entire body

Body is jointed at shoulders and hips

Coat conceals solidly stuffed torso and limbs

Thumb is separate from fingers, but cut from same piece of cloth

Feet and legs are painted to resemble boots

Silk trousers, jacket, and star-spangled vest

KAMKINS DOLL
(RIGHT) Louise R. Kampes designed these dolls, which were made in her Atlantic City, New Jersey, studios between 1919 and 1928. The head of this example is marked at the back, under the hairline "Kampes/Atlantic City." Ht: 18in (46cm)

Leather shoes

Clothes were made by out-workers to Mrs. Kampes's design

Painted and Sewn Dolls

· 1880s to 1900s ·

TOWARD THE END OF THE NINETEENTH century, many companies were making rag dolls in large quantities, although they still produced the dolls individually. The facial features were often sewn by hand: eyes, ears, noses, and mouths were stitched onto good-quality fabrics such as fine cotton, silk, and stockinette. A skilled needlewoman could create a fairly realistic face from a flat, moonlike surface. Alternatively, the dolls' facial features were hand painted in oil colors; sometimes they used a combination of painting and sewing.
By the turn of the century, rag dolls were more sophisticated. As is the case with Philadelphia Baby, shown here, the heads were often made of stockinette that had been stretched over a firm papier-mâché base and molded into shape. With its rigid head, this type of doll had painted, rather than sewn, facial features.

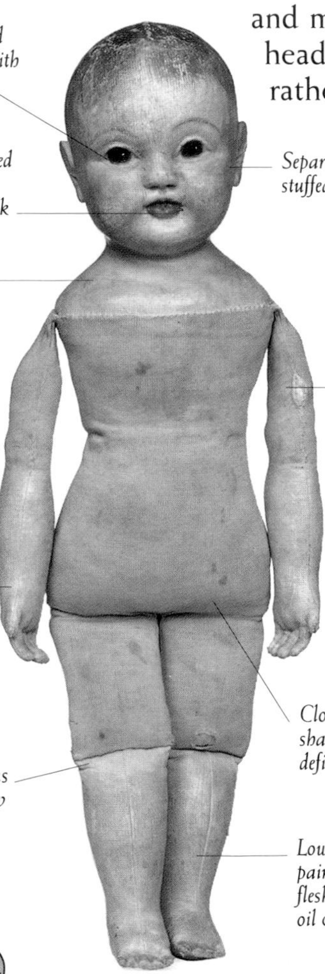

Brown painted hair worn away in places to reveal stockinette

Molded, well-defined features

Soft, rosy pink skin tones are painted onto face

Large, painted brown eyes with black pupils

Well-defined mouth, painted pink

Separate ears are stuffed and shaped

Sleeveless dress with embroidered anchor at neck

Shoulder head is painted in flesh-toned oil colors

Floppy arms are stitched to torso at shoulder seams

Sailor-style smock with blue and white striped trim and red bow

Lower arms, painted in flesh-toned oil colors

Cloth body, shaped to define waist

Five lifelike fingers stitched on each hand

Stitched seams at knees allow movement

Lower legs, painted in flesh-toned oil colors

PHILADELPHIA BABY *This is one of a line of Philadelphia Baby dolls produced c.1900 for J.B. Sheppard and Co., a department store in Philadelphia, Pennsylvania. The dolls varied in size from 18in (46cm) to 22in (55cm). The shoulder head and facial features are painted in oil colors, as are the lower arms and lower legs. It has a soft cloth body.*

Five toes stitched on each foot; no shoes

HT: 22in (55cm)

Solid head, made of strong calico, filled with hardwood

Stitching throws eyebrows and nose into relief

COBO DOLL (LEFT) Rag doll-makers Alice Le Hureys and Judy Guilles manufactured this model in Cobo, an area in Guernsey, in the Channel Islands, c.1900. Its facial features are crudely painted and stitched. Ht: 15in (37.5cm)

SANTA CLAUS (RIGHT) From the 1880s to c.1917, a type of doll known as worsted dolls began to be produced commercially. This example dates from c.1890, and was probably made by Emil Wittzack of Gotha in Thuringia, Germany. Ht: 14in (35cm)

Black bead eyes

Needle-stitched stockinette head

Lower arms, painted in flesh-colored tones

Hand-knitted, red and blue striped outfit

Brown cotton gift sack carried on Santa's back

Red and green woolen tassels, and metal bells

THE COLE FAMILY (BELOW) Roxanna Elizabeth McGee Cole started making dolls in the United States in 1868. She died in 1907, but her daughter-in-law, Molly Hunt Cole, took over the running of the business. This family of five was created c.1901, and is unique. All the dolls are made of fine muslin, which is hand-painted and delicately stitched.

Small bisque doll, carried in the crook of each arm

Flannel boots, stitched to gray trousers at knee

Lower legs, painted in flesh-colored tones

GRANDMA COLE
Ht: 22in (55cm)

THE MAID
Ht: 17½in (45cm)

BABY
Ht: 15in (38cm)

JOSIE JUNE
Ht: 17½in (45cm)

MAY
Ht: 17½in (45cm)

Typical maid's uniform: mobcap; apron; checked dress, and lace-up shoes

Long robe conceals flannel petticoat, diaper, and small white slippers; a wicker rattle is attached to baby's wrist

White, lacy dress and broad-brimmed bonnet; hair drawn in pencil and painted in watercolors; holds small bisque doll

Skirt and jacket, and blouse with lace fichu; accessories include reading glasses, knitting needles and wool; human hair is sewn on

Smock worn over gingham dress; cotton undergarments; holds small bisque doll

Printed Cloth Dolls

· 1900s to 1980s ·

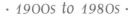

AS DEMAND FOR COMMERCIALLY made rag dolls increased, factories began to produce printed cloth dolls, sometimes known as cut-out cloth dolls. The front and back of each doll were printed onto cotton sheets. Then the sheet of cloth would be sold, ready to be cut out, sewn together, and stuffed with kapok, straw, or even sawdust by the buyer. These dolls represented a variety of characters – some were well known, such as a celebrity or storybook character; others represented types, such as a pretty girl or soldier.

Although the first printed cloth dolls were made in the last half of the nineteenth century, most of the dolls that survive were manufactured after 1900. The chromolithographic process caused the fabric to deteriorate, as did rough handling and washing; in some cases, the stuffing was eaten away by animals or insects.

Doll's name is printed on cap

Idealized features: "rosebud" mouth and large eyes

Outfit represents the Liberty Bell in Philadelphia

Patriotic stars and stripes on cap and T-shirt

Hanging loop attached at shoulder seams

Liberty Bell's crack reproduced on doll

Company name printed at base of bell

Printed cloth label shows limited-edition number (891)

All-in-one cloth body stuffed with kapok

MISS LIBERTY BELLE *Produced in 1976, this doll commemorates 200 years of American independence on the front of her dress, and 150 years of independence on the back. It is named after the Liberty Bell in Philadelphia, Pennsylvania. Printed by the Toy Works (Hodge Podge) in Massachusetts, it is a limited-edition doll.*

HT: 14½in (36.5cm)

Distinctive ponytail

Printed cloth body, prestuffed with kapok

"Tails" give an extra dimension to the doll

Cereal package features Sunny Jim character

RED RIDING HOOD

(RIGHT) This cut-out doll pattern was printed in the United States c.1970. For economic reasons, cut-out doll patterns were usually printed continuously onto a large piece of cloth, which was then sold by the yard (or meter). These shapes were printed on a cotton strip 18in (46cm) wide. Ht: 16½in (42cm)

Red cape is a separate cut-out shape

Design shows how doll should look after sewing

Front and back of doll to be stuffed and sewn up

Red kerchief

SUNNY JIM (LEFT) In 1905, A.C.
Fincken, the manufacturer of Force Wheat Flakes, a breakfast cereal launched in 1901 in the United States, issued a printed cloth doll to promote its product. Sunny Jim, a caricature of an early 1800s gentleman, could be obtained by sending coupons and a small sum of money to the manufacturer. Both Force Wheat Flakes and the doll are still available today. This model dates from c.1970. Ht: 16in (41cm)

STRUWWELPETER (RIGHT) This well-
known German storybook character, Struwwelpeter ("Shock-headed Peter"), was the creation of Dr. Heinrich Hoffmann. Since the publication of Hoffmann's cautionary tales in 1845, Struwwelpeter, the disobedient boy who refused to cut his hair or nails, has been portrayed in doll form many times. This printed cloth model was made in the Far East. Ht: 13in (33cm)

Yellow and beige wool sewn onto head

Facial features printed onto cloth

Fronts and backs of all four dolls printed on single sheet

PRINTED DOLLS

(LEFT) Printed onto a cotton sheet, the dolls are named Cora, Agnes, Sylvia, and May. They were designed by Samuel Finburgh and first printed in 1916. In the 1970s the designs were reprinted by Hulbert Fabrics A.U.L. for Her Majesty's Stationery Office, which supplied them to the Bethnal Green Museum of Childhood in London. Ht: 15½in (39cm)

Clothes based on the storybook illustration

Nails 1in (2.5cm) long are made of vinyl and glued onto cloth hands

Printed label indicates doll is copyright of Heinrich-Hoffmann-Museum GmbH

Steiff Dolls
· 1900s to the present day ·

THE STEIFF COMPANY, established by Margarete Steiff in 1877, is still in business today. Although probably best known for its teddy bears, it also produced a wide range of dolls and other stuffed toys. These two pages show a selection of Steiff rag dolls made in the early 1900s. Steiff dolls of this period were usually made of felt, and the range of characters they portrayed was diverse. Many were caricatures of types, such as policemen, circus entertainers, or sailors, with exaggerated and often comical features. Some represented storybook characters.

Distinguishing features of Steiff dolls include a center or diagonal seam on the face, and the company's "Button-in-Ear" trademark (see Doll Marks, opposite). If the button is missing from the doll, there are usually telltale signs where it was once punched through the felt.

Shiny black shoe-button eyes sewn into face

Smile indicated with red paint

Limp gray mohair sewn to head

Socket head, made of molded felt

Unpainted cloth body, jointed at shoulders

Posture of old woman: drooping bustline, sagging stomach, and rounded shoulders

Jointed hips allow some movement

Thumb is separate from fingers, but cut from the same piece of cloth

Large hands appear rather swollen

Knees are fixed in a bent position

Large feet; no toes

OLD WOMAN *First marketed in 1913, this doll was reissued in the late 1980s. It is an unusually life-like portrayal of an elderly woman with sagging posture. The legs are the most startling feature: bent and gnarled, they even show traces of varicose veins.*

HT: 19in (48cm)

Wide mouth is stitched and painted red

Curly white mohair plush hair extends around the back of the head

Shirt decorated with red bow tie at neck and small black buttons

Blue felt suit trimmed with ribbed brass buttons

Large, round felt patches represent spectacles

Back of Steiff button is visible in left ear

Black shoe-button eyes sewn onto felt spectacles

HEAD DETAIL (ABOVE) Available between 1905 and 1914, this all-felt doll bears a Steiff metal button in its ear (see Doll Marks, right). These buttons were usually attached to the doll's left ear and could face either forward or backward.

Hands in clenched fist position; fingers indicated by stitching

DOLL MARKS

"Button-in-Ear" was registered as a trademark in May 1905.

~

Dolls made after 1905 bear a metal button marked "STEIFF" in raised lettering (see below).

~

In 1908–1909 a cloth label, printed with the product number, was attached to the metal button.

~

From 1926 a chest label was added to Steiff dolls.

GROSSPAPA (LEFT) With his white hair and knobby knees, Grosspapa (or Grandpapa) clearly represents an elderly man. His upright posture and clenched fists indicate that he is a proud and robust character. Ht: 14½in (37cm)

Felt legs are also intended to be trousers

Long, pointed shoes, worn with felt spats, are made of brown leather

Blond mohair plush hair, sewn onto head and clipped short

Nostrils are painted red for realistic effect

Lips and flesh tones are tinted soft red

Green felt suspenders, embroidered with yellow chainstitching

Fingers indicated by beige mercerized cotton thread

Shaped fingers and thumbs

Characteristic Steiff seam down center of face

Seams on either side of the eyes give doll interesting expression

"Button-in-Ear" faces backward

Lips made of a separate piece of felt sewn in and painted

Felt breeches, trimmed with chainstitch, are tied at knee

"GEORGE" (LEFT) Steiff's trade name for this model was actually Hans, but this particular doll was renamed "George" by its owner. An all-felt construction, the doll is similar to Anthony (right), but twice the size. Ht: 24in (60cm)

ANTHONY (LEFT) Made by Steiff in 1909, Anthony was distributed by Borgfeldt in the United States. It was available in five sizes, from 11in (28cm) to 24in (60cm), some models contained a voice box in the torso. The traditional Tyrolean costume is completely original, and made of good-quality materials. Ht: 11in (28cm)

English Manufacturers

· 1920s to 1950s ·

BETWEEN 1920 AND 1940, RAG DOLLS enjoyed a new wave of popularity. Working at the same time as Lenci in Italy and Käthe Kruse in Germany (see pages 100–101), English companies produced many new models of rag dolls in quantity for the domestic and international markets. These represented a wide range of character types. Often they were made as souvenirs, portraying a famous figure such as a new king. One of the most successful English companies to make rag dolls was Chad Valley Co. Ltd. Originally a printing firm called Johnson Brothers, it was established c.1850 in Birmingham. The firm was renamed Chad Valley in 1897, and diversified to manufacture games, jigsaw puzzles, and stuffed toys. The first dolls were produced c.1920.

Reddish brown mohair is sewn on to form a side part

Facial features molded from stiffened felt and painted

Socket head is made of firmly stuffed felt

Kapok-stuffed calico body, jointed at shoulders and hips

Velvet arms, covered by the cotton uniform

Separate, but not applied, thumb

Hands are stitched to indicate fingers

Shiny black American-cloth shoes

Cotton dress is part of the doll's structure and cannot be removed

American-cloth trim on cuffs and collar

Hygienic Toys label attached to right wrist

Cotton stockings conceal velvet legs

The label, tied to the right wrist, indicates that the doll is safe for children.

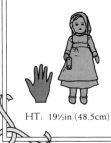

HT: 19½in (48.5cm)

CHAD VALLEY CO. LTD., NURSE *A fine example of a Chad Valley doll, this model was first issued c.1930. The Hygienic Toys/Seal of Purity label indicates that this model is made of safe, good-quality materials. It distinguishes the doll from many Eastern European imports made during this period, which contained sawdust, moss, or animal hair.*

DEAN'S RAG BOOK CO. LTD., LUPINO LANE (*LEFT*) The wire-frame base, covered with padding, is completely flexible and allows the limbs of this 1939 doll to be bent into different positions. Lupino Lane was the star of the musical Me and My Girl. Ht: 12½in (31.5cm)

This printed label is attached to the sole of the doll's right foot.

Label indicates actor's name and song from the musical

Woolen checked suit is part of body structure

Doll's limbs are completely flexible

CHAD VALLEY CO. LTD., SEVEN DWARFS (*BELOW*) In 1937, Walt Disney released its animated cartoon Snow White and the Seven Dwarfs. In 1938, Chad Valley produced the characters from the cartoon in doll form. The faces are individually molded from felt and painted, giving each dwarf a unique facial expression and personality. Ht: 6½in (16.5cm)
© The Walt Disney Company

MERRYTHOUGHT LTD., SLEEPY AND HAPPY (*ABOVE and RIGHT*) Merrythought was founded in 1930, and is still in business to this day. In the mid-1950s, the firm made a set of Walt Disney's Snow White and the Seven Dwarfs. Ht: 10in (24.5cm)
© The Walt Disney Company

SLEEPY

"Happy" features painted onto molded felt face

HAPPY

Fingers indicated with stitching; separate, but not applied, thumb

J.K. FARNELL AND CO. LTD., H.M. THE KING (*RIGHT*) J.K. Farnell was established as a toy-maker c. 1870 in Acton, London, and began producing dolls in 1915. This doll, made in 1937, commemorated the coronation of George VI, after the abdication of his brother, Edward VIII. Ht: 15in (38cm)

The label is attached under the doll's right pocket flap.

Black teased-wool bearskin, with 2in- (5cm) high woolen plume

Facial features molded from stiffened felt and painted

Costume is replica of Royal Highlanders' uniform

Metal sword painted black with gold tip

White plush sporran with black braid tassels

A label, attached to the sole of the foot, bears the name of the manufacturer

A woven label, concealed by the jacket, is sewn to the body of each dwarf shown below.

DOPEY   GRUMPY   BASHFUL   DOC   HAPPY

SNEEZY   SLEEPY

Trousers are part of the legs   Removable felt jackets   Pink cotton bodies and backs of heads   Label reads, "THIS IS HAPPY"

European Manufacturers

· 1920s to 1950s ·

BY THE 1920s, several European manufacturers were producing very high-quality rag dolls. Sometimes known as "art dolls," these were often designed and painted by talented artists, and modeled by highly skilled craftsmen. German doll-maker Käthe Kruse and the Italian firm Lenci were two of the leading manufacturers of rag dolls. Both of these companies are still in business.

Käthe Kruse, wife of sculptor Max Kruse, was a talented painter; she began making dolls c.1911. Convinced that bisque dolls were not practical toys, she decided that her dolls would be unbreakable and easy to play with. Lenci was founded in Turin in 1918 by Elena Scavini. It is thought that she named the firm after her own pet name, Lenci.

Side-glancing, painted brown eyes, with black pupils

Nostrils are painted in red

Typical Lenci mouth is closed and painted in red

Reddish blond mohair is sewn onto head

Boyish features are molded and painted

Separate, shaped ears

Socket head made of stiffened felt

Two fingers are joined on hand; typical Lenci feature

Smock was made at same time as doll

Torso, like the head, is made of stiffened and molded felt

Joints at shoulders and hips allow some movement

Piglet is a 1950s copy of the toy made for author A.A. Milne's son, the original Christopher Robin

LENCI, BOY *Made in the 1920s, this is a fine example of a Lenci doll. Although it bears a remarkable resemblance to E.H. Shepard's illustrations of Christopher Robin, the hero of A.A. Milne's famous Pooh Bear stories, there is no evidence to suggest that Lenci modeled the doll on this character. It is extremely lifelike, and has a charming, slightly wary expression.*

HT: 19in (47.5cm)

Black plush hair, sewn on

Molded bulbous eyes; right eye is partly closed

LENCI, BELLBOY (LEFT) This bellboy character, made by Lenci c.1920, was available as a black or white doll. The number identifies this doll as a fairly early Lenci model: the model numbers began with 100 and passed 2000 by 1930. The small button attached to the bellboy's cuff is the first style of Lenci button produced. Ht: 11in (28cm)

Highlights painted in white onto iris

LENCI, GIRL (LEFT) This c.1922 doll has typical Lenci features: brown painted eyes looking to the side, a small, rosebud mouth, and a rather sullen expression. Lenci designs are very distinctive; however, the untagged dolls are often quite difficult to identify, as other manufacturers tended to imitate many of the company's designs. Ht: 12½in (32cm)

All-in-one cotton and lace undergarment

Raised, molded button attached to left cuff reads "Lenci"

Fingers are indicated by stitches; separate thumb, but cut from same piece of fabric

Shaped fingers and thumbs; stitching indicates gloves

Red felt suit

Original cream felt dress, trimmed with dark turquoise felt

This metal button, attached to the doll's undergarment, is the second style of Lenci button produced.

Black oilcloth shoes, with white felt spats

Characteristic three seam lines at back of head

Human hair wig; hairs are sewn onto a thin silk skullcap, three at a time

Molded and painted face intended to resemble that of a child as closely as possible

C-shaped ears applied to head separately

KÄTHE KRUSE, BABY (RIGHT) It is said that Käthe Kruse made her first doll from a potato and a towel filled with sand. By 1911, she was producing high-quality rag dolls in quantity. The construction of this 1920s baby doll is complicated; it has been assembled from numerous panels of cloth, which have been sewn together. Ht: 16in (41cm)

Dress conceals cloth body and limbs, stuffed with a soft but hard-wearing filling

MAGDA BOALT, SWEDISH DOLL

(RIGHT) Sometimes known as the Swedish Käthe Kruse, Magda Boalt is probably Scandinavia's best-known doll-maker. A one-time hairdresser, she began by making small wigs for dolls, using remnants of human hair. In 1944, she made her first doll. This model was manufactured c.1950. Ht: 19in (48cm)

Wrist originally bore a label with doll's name

Body has two seams at front and back; five-panel leg construction

Black leather shoes, with metal buckles

Foot is lined with stiff paper and stamped with product number

Norah Wellings

· 1919 to 1960 ·

NORAH WELLINGS BEGAN HER CAREER in 1919 with the Chad Valley Co. Ltd. (see pages 98–99). In 1926, she opened her own factory, Victoria Toy Works, in Shropshire, England, where she designed and made dolls until 1960. During this time, she also designed dolls for Chad Valley. For this reason, many dolls produced by these two firms are quite similar. However, those manufactured at the Norah Wellings factory can be identified by a woven label sewn to the body (see Doll Marks, opposite).
~ Norah Wellings dolls are generally made of felt, velvet, and velveteen, and represent children and adults. She produced many ethnic dolls as well as numerous storybook characters. Probably the finest Norah Wellings dolls were made in the 1930s.

Heart-shaped face molded from stiffened felt

Side-glancing blue eyes, painted in oil colors

Two red painted dots accentuate the nostrils

Reddish brown mohair is sewn to head

Swivel head is turned to side

Orange, peasant-style felt dress with laced bodice

Shoulder joints allow some movement

Original wooden-bead bracelets, attached to both wrists, cannot be removed

Only two fingers sewn together, an unusual feature

Jointed at hips to allow movement

Legs are shaped to define calves and ankles

Toes indicated by stitching; label sewn to base of left foot

Orange felt shoes, with metal buttons

ORANGE GIRL This large, 1930s felt doll has a swivel head. The body is stuffed and jointed at the shoulders and hips, and the facial features are molded and painted. The hands are of special interest, as only two of the fingers are joined together. Usually, the fingers of Norah Wellings dolls are indicated by stitching, with a separate thumb.

HT: 17½in (44cm)

SAILORS (LEFT) These c.1928
dolls were sold on board passenger
liners as souvenirs. They were made
in two styles: "grinning" sailors
(top), with felt feet and large,
protruding, pointed ears; and
"smiling" sailors (bottom),
with velvet feet and flat
ears. Ht: 8½in (21cm)

Hat, stamped
with name of ship

Woven label, sewn
to sole of left foot

Felt flowers
worn in hair

ORIENTAL GIRL (LEFT) This
1930s all-felt doll is not merely a
standard model dressed in
oriental clothing. The face has
been carefully designed to
portray specific ethnic
characteristics; the coloring is
as true to life as possible. A
Norah Wellings label is sewn
to the foot. Ht: 12½in (31cm)

Fingers are indicated
by stitching;
separate thumb

Felt Japanese-
style kimono

Woven label sewn
to sole of right foot

HARRY THE HAWK (BELOW)
During World War II, Norah
Wellings made dolls representing
characters from the Army, Royal
Navy, and Royal Air Force. This
mascot doll, Harry the Hawk, raised
funds for men serving in the Royal
Air Force (R.A.F.) during the war.
Ht: 7in (18cm)

Felt parachute, in
patriotic colors

Label indicates that
the R.A.F. benefits
from sales of the doll

Brown felt intended
to represent leather
gauntlets

Outfit is based on
authentic R.A.F.
flying combat
coveralls

GUARDSMEN (RIGHT) Like the sailors
shown above, two styles of guardsmen
dolls were available: those that grin,
and those that smile. Both wear the
same uniform, and were made in a
range of sizes, some as large as 36in
(91cm). These models were made in
the 1930s. Ht: Largest 33½in
(84.5cm); smallest 10in (25cm)

Colored-velvet
uniforms are part
of doll's body

DOLL MARKS
Sewn-on cloth labels were
firmly stitched to Norah
Wellings dolls.

~

The labels are black, blue,
or beige, depending on the
color of the doll.

MADE IN ENGLAND
BY
NORAH WELLINGS

Labels are usually sewn to
the foot, but can appear on
the wrist or on the doll's back.

MADE IN ENGLAND
BY
NORAH WELLINGS

Celluloid Dolls

In the last quarter of the nineteenth century, celluloid began to compete with the traditional materials used in doll-making, such as bisque, wood, paper, and cloth. It was a versatile substance, made from pyroxylin (cellulose nitrates) and camphor. Economical and easy to produce, celluloid was used extensively for the manufacturing of dolls, as well as many household items, until the mid-1950s, when it was superseded by other plastics.

CELLULOID WAS DEVELOPED and first used for dolls by the Hyatt Brothers of New Jersey, in the late 1860s. Their firm registered the name "celluloid" in 1869, and worked under a new name, the Celluloid Novelty Company. Although the product was patented, the word celluloid is often used to describe all types of pyroxylin mixtures, regardless of the manufacturer.

∾ Celluloid was not only manufactured for the doll-making industry. A number of companies in Europe and the United States made celluloid as a substitute for many natural materials, such as tortoiseshell, bone, ivory, coral, and even marble. It was made into a variety of items, from eyeglass frames and hair clips to billiard balls, teething rings, children's bathtime toys, dice, and rulers.

∾ Celluloid dolls were manufactured by placing the substance in its solid state into a two-piece metal mold. Steam or hot air was then blown into the mold under pressure; this would soften the celluloid and cause it to conform to the shape, and bond the two halves of the molded celluloid. When cool, the mold was removed and the doll was decorated.

Mass-produced Celluloid Dolls

When celluloid was first used for dolls at the end of the nineteenth century, it was a relatively expensive material. By the first quarter of the twentieth century, it had become extremely cheap to produce. Factories

CLAUDINET AND CLAUDINE
(LEFT) Advertised in a French catalog in 1937, this pair of dolls is fashionably and expensively dressed; both sets of clothing show smocking on the yokes. They were available individually or as a pair. Ht: Claudinet 25½in (64cm); Claudine 23in (57cm)

MINIATURE KEWPIE *(RIGHT) This all-celluloid Kewpie doll was probably made in the United States or Germany during the 1930s. The knobs of hair and facial features are molded and painted, and it bears blue wings, characteristic of many Kewpie models, on its back. The doll is marked "Design 43980 Patent." Ht: 2in (5cm)*

BOAT RACE FAVOR (LEFT)

In 1939, spectators at England's University Boat Race could buy a small novelty doll, or "favor," dressed in the color of their team's crew: Oxford was dark blue, Cambridge was light blue. This small celluloid doll, probably made in Japan, is an Oxford favor. It wears a pom-pom and carries a pair of oars. The safety pin was used to attach the doll to the supporter's clothing. Ht: 3in (7.5cm)

in Germany, France, the United States, and Japan were producing celluloid dolls by the thousands. Famous manufacturers of celluloid dolls include: the Rheinische Gummi- und Celluloid-Fabrik and J.D. Kestner in Germany; Petitcollin in France; the Wilson Doll Company in England; and the Averill Manufacturing Company, E.I. Horsman, Parsons–Jackson, and the Celluloid Novelty Company in the United States.

Most of the celluloid dolls produced in Europe were manufactured in Germany. Probably the best known factory was the Rheinische Gummi- und Celluloid-Fabrik, founded in 1873. Products made by this company can usually be recognized by the famous turtle-in-a-diamond trademark (see pages 106–107). In addition to producing celluloid dolls, this company also made celluloid heads for other

manufacturers, exactly as the porcelain factories made and sold heads of bisque. The heads were sent to companies within Germany, and to England and the United States, where they were attached to stuffed or composition bodies. Manufacturers who assembled dolls from component parts made by the Rheinische Gummi- und Celluloid-Fabrik included Kämmer and Reinhardt, C. and O. Dressel, and J.D. Kestner.

The End of the Celluloid Era

In many ways, celluloid was a very suitable material for doll-making. It was light, and easy to mold and decorate. However, it was extremely flammable, which was naturally of great concern worldwide. A less serious problem was that it faded in bright light, which meant that the features became bleached with time. It was easily crushed if the doll was stepped on, or even squeezed tightly. If poor-quality celluloid was used, as was often the case in the 1930s and 1940s, it was thin and disintegrated quickly. With the invention of plastics in the mid-1950s, celluloid was replaced by safer, more reliable materials, such as vinyl.

TYROLEAN PAIR (RIGHT)

The turtle trademark on the dolls' backs and the wrist tags indicate that this pair was made for Käthe Kruse by the Rheinische Gummi- und Celluloid-Fabrik in the early 1950s. The boy has sleeping eyes with lashes; the girl has molded, painted eyes. Ht: Boy 16in (40cm); girl 15½in (39cm)

JAPANESE BOXER (LEFT)

Like most Japanese celluloid dolls mass-produced in the 1930s, this figure is small, brittle, and cheaply made. Japanese celluloids made at this time were often amusing trinkets or novelty items produced for the West, rather than for the Japanese market. Ht: 4in (10cm)

German Manufacturers

· 1870s to 1960s ·

ESTABLISHED IN BAVARIA in 1873 by Friedrich Bensinger, the Rheinische Gummi- und Celluloid-Fabrik was the major producer of celluloid in Germany. Today, the company produces vinyl dolls from its original factory in Mannheim–Neckarau; since the early 1950s, it has operated under the name Schildkröt-Spielwaren GmbH. ⁓ Schildkröte is the German word for "turtle," and the company's main trademark was a walking turtle encased in a diamond, which was molded on the doll necks and bodies. The mark is raised. In some cases the diamond is omitted, or the turtle is enclosed in a circle, square, oval, triangle, or hexagon. Other manufacturers of celluloid also used the trademark of a turtle to represent durability; however, the raised turtle-in-a-diamond was exclusive to the Rheinische Gummi- und Celluloid-Fabrik.

The turtle mark and model number and signature of Käthe Kruse appear on the back of the doll.

Inset blue glass eyes

Molded nose; nostrils painted in red

Molded and painted brown hair

Eyebrows are painted in brown

Head and torso molded as one; head cannot turn

Celluloid body, jointed at shoulders

Straight arms are shaped to define elbows

Dress has small orange-red bow at neck of cape collar

Blue cotton dress conceals white one-piece undergarment

Jointed hips allow some movement

Molded fingers, with separate thumbs

Straight legs are shaped to define knees

Feet point inward; molded toes

Wrist tag, with turtle-in-a-diamond trademark

Cream machine-knitted socks

KÄTHE KRUSE, BLUE-DRESS GIRL *In the mid-1950s, Käthe Kruse worked with the Rheinische Gummi- und Celluloid-Fabrik to produce all-celluloid dolls, and dolls made of Tortulon — a new plastic that resembled hard vinyl. This model is made entirely of celluloid, yet manages to retain the facial characteristics of a Käthe Kruse rag doll (see pages 100–101).*

Red leather shoes with metal buckles

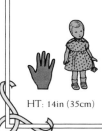

HT: 14in (35cm)

BUSCHOW AND BECK, BOY

(RIGHT) Buschow and Beck, famous for its doll heads, was founded in Silesia, Germany, in 1888. This figure, made in the 1920s, has a celluloid head and cloth body, and may be a Käthe Kruse design. Ht: 12in (30cm).

The head mark bears the helmet trademark, mold number, and size number.

Molded hair, painted brown

Celluloid socket head can turn

Cloth torso, jointed at shoulders

Joints at hips and shoulders allow some movement of limbs

Cloth limbs, stuffed with excelsior

Toes are indicated by stitching

Feet are made from separate piece of fabric

MADAME HENDREN, BOY

(RIGHT) Madame Hendren was the trade name used between 1915 and 1965 for dolls that were designed and patented by Madame Georgene Averill and made by the Averill Manufacturing Co. of New York City. Ht: 18in (46cm).

Celluloid head is molded with turtle-in-a-diamond mark on the back

Peach cotton smock conceals cloth body

Oddly shaped, irregular teeth

The cloth body is stamped "GENUINE 'MADAME HENDREN' DOLL/1920/ MADE IN U.S.A."

Composition limbs; flesh-colored paint is flaking off in some places

J.D. KESTNER, GIRL

(LEFT) This doll, with a celluloid shoulder head, kid body, and bisque lower arms, was made by Kestner c.1915. The body is a fine example of the high-quality kid bodies made in Germany at the time. Ht: 18in (16cm)

Light brown mohair wig

Manufacturer's trademark, attached to kid torso

Lead pin joints at elbows and shoulders

Lower arms and tiny hands are made of bisque

Hinged joints at hips and knees

The mark is incised on the shoulder head of the doll.

The paper label indicates that the body is stuffed with cork.

TURTLE-MARK BOY

(LEFT) Made in Germany in the 1930s, this naked boy doll is a typical product of the Rheinische Gummi- und Celluloid-Fabrik. All the facial features are painted. Ht: 10½in (26.5cm)

Molded hair, painted blond

Head and torso molded as one; head does not turn

The raised turtle mark on the back of the head identifies the manufacturer.

Bent arms with molded hands

Body is jointed at hips and shoulders

Legs are molded with dimpled knees

Five molded toes on each foot

Mass-produced Dolls

· 1900s to 1980s ·

FROM THE 1900S TO MID-1950S, millions of celluloid dolls were produced. Some were good quality, such as those manufactured by the Rheinische Gummi-und Celluloid-Fabrik, but many were quite poorly made. Throughout the 1920s and 1930s, celluloid novelty dolls were very popular. Cheap and cheerful, these little trinkets were usually mass-produced in Japan and given away as carnival prizes, or sold at the seashore for a small sum.

By the mid-1950s, doll manufacturers in Germany, the United States, France, and England had stopped using celluloid for dolls, owing to its flammability. Instead, they preferred to work with new and safer plastics, such as vinyl. In some Eastern European countries, such as Poland, celluloid dolls continued to be produced until the late 1980s.

The "K" trademark identifies the doll manufacturer, Kaliskie Zaklady.

Upper eyelashes made of black nylon bristle; lower lashes painted in brown

Dark brown nylon wig, in fashionable style of the day

Hair tied at back of neck with green nylon ribbon

Checked-cotton mini-dress in style of 1960s–1970s

Socket head allows head to turn

Plump upper arms; jointed at shoulders

Molded fingers are slightly webbed; separate thumb

Rounded stomach of a toddler

Bent lower arms with molded hands

Straight legs are sturdy and thick-set

Center seams visible on legs

Small feet with indistinct, molded toes

POLISH DOLL, BEATA This all-celluloid toddler doll was produced by the Polish manufacturer Kaliskie Zaklady in the 1960s or 1970s — at least a decade after the West had ceased making celluloid dolls. The doll is otherwise composed of modern materials: the sleeping eyes are made of plastic, and the wig is nylon.

HT: 10½in (27cm)

Fashionable, slip-on PVC shoes

The raised mark on the back of the doll shows Petitcollin's trademark of an eagle's head.

Molded and painted mouth, eyes, and nose

Black doll with movable limbs

Fine organdy apron trimmed with gold ribbon and white lace

Full, checked-cotton skirt with gold ribbon trim

Molded and painted ribbed stockings and shoes

Crudely painted facial features

Bright pink pom-pom hair

Betty Boop look-alike

Lead weight in base makes doll bounce back up

NOVELTY DOLLS (ABOVE) *These novelty dolls were made in Japan in the 1920s and 1930s. The figure on the right is a tumbling doll. If it is pushed over, it will bounce back up again. Ht: Largest 2½in (6cm); smallest 2in (4.5cm)*

FRENCH COSTUME DOLL (LEFT)
Dressed in French provincial costume, this doll was made in the 1920s by the Petitcollin company of Paris, founded in 1914. The costume is highly ornate, but the doll itself is made of thin, rather brittle celluloid. Ht: 8½in (22cm)

Molded "earphone" hairstyle; hair painted blond

Inset blue glass eyes; painted brows

Dress made c.1960; the fabric is possibly older

Well-formed hands, with separate fingers and thumbs

"Foreign" usually indicates that a doll was made in Japan.

Molded hair; faint signs of paint remain

Two black dots indicate eyes; no lashes

Molded, closed mouth is crudely painted

Mold cast lines have not been cleaned

JAPANESE PAIR (RIGHT)
Mass-produced in Japan in the 1920s and 1930s, these small figures are low-quality, all-celluloid dolls. The facial features are molded and crudely painted, and much of the dolls' color has now faded. Ht: Largest 5in (12.5cm); smallest 2in (4.5cm)

GERMAN DOLL
(RIGHT) *With its blue eyes, blond hair, and tidy appearance, this doll reflects the 1930s Germanic ideal. The turtle-in-a-diamond trademark indicates that it was made by the Rheinische Gummi- und Celluloid-Fabrik. Ht: 15½in (38.5cm)*

Well-shaped celluloid limbs

Modern Dolls

*Although some American composition dolls made in the early twentieth century were thought
almost revolutionary at the time, the real "modern" era in the history of dolls begins
in the 1940s — the decade that saw the start of the plastics boom and the move to production
on a massive scale. Yet not all modern dolls are plastic, nor are they all mass-produced.
The past 50 years have seen an extraordinarily wide range of models being made.*

WORLD WAR II HAD A PROFOUND impact on doll manufacturing in Europe. Suddenly, most production ceased in areas where an industry had built up over centuries. When peace did return, it brought with it revolutionary new plastics – developed to help the war effort and now available for all types of applications.

Light, strong, and easily molded into an infinite variety of forms, the new plastic materials demanded new equipment and new technologies for production. Although the initial investment costs were very high, manufacturers found that they could produce millions of dolls that were all identical, or create a line of dolls based on the same basic model, making only minor modifications to give each doll its characteristic features.

Plastic dolls of the late 1940s are vastly different from those of today. They were made of hard plastic and, although they looked like the composition dolls they largely replaced, they were lighter, tougher, and more durable. The arrival of the polyethylene compounds followed, introduced in the mid-1950s. Commonly referred to as vinyl, it is a much more flexible material, available in both hard and soft forms.

The Difference with Vinyl

Vinyl brought a key difference to doll hair: while composition and hard plastic dolls had wigs, or molded and painted hair, the use of soft vinyl allowed hair to be "rooted" into the head. Facial features, hands, and feet tend to be less well molded, and less defined in vinyl dolls than in those made of composition or hard plastic. Most dolls today use a combination of vinyls: soft for the head and limbs, and hard for the body.

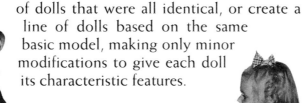

SELLING SHIRLEY *(RIGHT) An illustration from the Sears, Roebuck mail order catalog advertises the latest Shirley Temple doll. The catalog dates from 1939, when dolls were just beginning to be mass-produced on a grand scale.*

SHOPPING FOR CLOTHES *(LEFT) A saleswoman at Harrods in London in the 1950s helps a young customer choose clothing for her doll. This personal approach to selling is in marked contrast to the aggressive marketing techniques of later 20th-century decades.*

WAAC-ETTE

WAVE ETTE

PATRIOTIC DOLLS (*LEFT*) *In 1943, Vogue Dolls in the United States issued these two dolls, representing women serving in the wartime army and navy. After the war, doll manufacturing changed dramatically. Ht: 13in (33cm)*

of doll-makers Lynne and Michael Roche (see pages 81 and 128), dolls are still created by the traditional methods. Only a few of each model are produced, and wood or other natural materials take the place of modern synthetics. These dolls are usually classified as art dolls – to be displayed rather than played with as toys by children.

Popular Appeal

The popularity of modern dolls tends to be much more transient than that of their predecessors. New models come and go continually as the power of advertising and the influence of the media, especially films and television, encourage fads and fashions that change virtually overnight.

～ While the charm of many traditional models guarantees their continuing appeal, novelty dolls are very much in demand: from character dolls drawn from cartoons and comic books, like the Batman and Robin models shown below, to baby dolls with ever more realistic features (see pages 122–123). But the great commercial successes of the age are the "dressing" dolls, especially those that are available with not only changes of clothing, but also with every conceivable accessory. Mattel's Barbie (see pages 116–117), which truly embodies the "more-is-better" values of today's society, is produced at a rate of 55,000 a day; 600 million have been sold since the doll's launch in 1959.

Strong competition and financial difficulties have forced the closure of many of the small individual companies that survived the war years; today most doll manufacturers belong to giant corporations. Over the past 20 years even these have been forced to merge or close down completely. Usually, the most marketable products have been sold, either as a profit-making concern, or in name only: the Sindy doll, for example, was once an English product made by Pedigree, but is now owned by the American company Hasbro (see pages 120–121).

Small-scale Producers

Doll-making, in contrast to large corporate enterprise, survives as a cottage industry to this day. Across the world, in studios and workshops, such as those

ROBIN

BATMAN

SUPERMAN

THREE SUPERHEROES (*RIGHT*)
This famous trio has all the right ingredients for success in the 1990s market: the dolls are based on hugely popular comic book characters; they are fully jointed for imaginative play; and they have their own accessories.
Batman, Robin, & Superman ™ & © 1993 DC Comics. All rights reserved.

Vogue Dolls, Inc.

· 1940s to 1960s ·

JENNIE GRAVES was already established as a designer and producer of fine dolls' clothing when she founded Vogue Dolls, Inc., in 1948. Since the 1930s, she had purchased American- and German-made undressed dolls, clothed them with her own creations, and sold them through stores nationwide; but in 1948, she introduced Ginny, a doll of her own design. Other dolls were added – each with its own personalized accessories and outfits based on contemporary fashions – to create the Ginny Doll Family. The line included Ginnette (Ginny's baby sister), Jill (her older sister), and Jeff, who could be either Jill's boyfriend or the two sisters' brother. Every doll that was created represented the company's family tradition of producing quality dolls "that are made to be loved."

Light brown corduroy hat, trimmed with blue satin

Brown sleeping eyes, with painted brows and lower lashes

Closed mouth, painted red

Elephant-shaped blue buttons cover the hook-and-eye fastenings

Light brown corduroy jacket and skirt, lined with blue satin

Upper eyelashes are made of animal hair

Auburn mohair wig

Composition head and body, jointed only at neck, shoulders, and hips

Black and gold "Vogue" label stuck on skirt

Hands are molded into an expressive up-and-outward attitude

Legs are quite straight below the knee, but have shapely thighs

Skating costume covers a blue satin all-in-one undergarment

Feet are flat and stubby, with no instep

White socks just visible inside skates

THE SKATER *This 1947 doll wears Vogue clothes designed by Jennie Graves, but predates the original Ginny. It has the same all-composition construction as the first Ginnies, which were somewhat shorter, standing only 8in (20cm) tall. The Skater is one of a group that represents various sporting activities: there is also a skier, a golfer, and a tennis player.*

Paperlike white cloth skates have metal blades

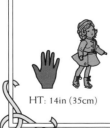

HT: 14in (35cm)

Synthetic wig, made of Dynel

Head turns from side to side when doll is "walked"

Molded and painted hair

Body is jointed only at shoulders and hips

White flannel dress jacket

Red painted finger- and toenails

Cummerbund around waist matches bow tie

Jill's corsage, trimmed with a pink bow, matches her dress

Trousers embellished with satin tuxedo stripe

Seamed thigh-high stockings

Black and silver glittery socks

Clear plastic open-toe high-heel shoes decorated with sparkles

Black plastic shoes, fastened with ribbon

DOLL MARKS

Dolls made from 1948 have a raised mark across the upper or lower back.

JILL
VOGUE DOLLS
INC.
MADE IN U.S.A
C 1957

A printed cloth label was sewn inside clothes after the company was incorporated.

Vogue Dolls Inc.

Wrist tags may also carry the legend "Ginny Doll Family/FASHION LEADERS IN DOLL SOCIETY."

I'm Ginny hi!

Vogue Dolls. INC.

JILL AND JEFF (LEFT) In his smart evening clothes, Jeff is all set to escort his friend – or sister – Jill to their high-school prom. The dolls are models that were both copyrighted in 1957. They are made of hard vinyl, and have blue sleeping eyes, with molded lashes and painted eyebrows. Ht: Jill 9¾in (24.5cm); Jeff 10in (25cm)

Body made of beige nylon plush fabric

Felt ears

Glass eyes

Printed tartan overcoat, labeled "GINNY'S PUP"

GINNY'S PUP (ABOVE) This miniature toy terrier is one of the many accessories made especially for Ginny. Ht: 3½in (9cm)

Untinted, molded curls on forehead and around face

Golden brown sleeping eyes, with molded lashes

Wig made of black Dynel

Separate thumb fits into the doll's mouth

All-composition Ginny doll model, jointed at shoulders and hips

GINNETTE (RIGHT) Made in the 1960s of tinted soft vinyl, Ginnette has the typical dumpy limbs of a baby doll, and a nursing mouth designed to take a feeding bottle or the doll's thumb. Ht: 8in (20cm)

Rounded, dimpled bent limbs

MISS 2000 (LEFT) The "Half-Century Group" was designed between 1948 and 1950. It featured the futuristically clad Miss 2000 and the Misses 1900, 1910, 1920, 1930, 1940, and 1950. A complete set is a real find. Ht: 8in (20cm)

Reverse of wrist tag

Ginny Doll Family
FASHION LEADERS IN DOLL SOCIETY

Front of wrist tag reads "Hi! I'm Ginnette/Created by VOGUE DOLLS Incorporated, Malden, Mass."

Both shoes are stamped on sole "Ginnette/Made in USA"

MISS 2000

American Manufacturers

· 1900s to the present day ·

A NUMBER OF DOLL MANUFACTURERS were established in the United States throughout the first quarter of the twentieth century, and some of them survive today in one form or another. Most of these manufacturers gained international reputations for their production or design of composition dolls – expertise that they later skillfully adapted to suit the new and exciting potential of plastic.

The Ideal Novelty and Toy Company of Brooklyn, New York, got off to a flying start when founders Morris Michtom and A. Cohn launched their "unbreakable" composition dolls. During the 1930s, Ideal issued a number based on famous film personalities: its Shirley Temple line, in particular, was extremely successful. After World War II, Ideal used its skills to create dolls made of all kinds of plastic; many were best-sellers.

Curly nylon "Shirley Temple" wig

Sleeping plastic eyes, with nylon upper lashes

Reverse socket head

Shoulder joints allow arms to rotate

Middle fingers of right hand are molded together

Straight legs, with shapely thighs

Flat feet allow the doll to stand unaided

Facial features are modeled on those of Shirley Temple

Smiling open mouth, with teeth

Slightly bent arms

Joints at hips allow movement of legs

Body is all-vinyl construction

Molded toes, with toenail detail

Genuine woven straw hat

Gold-colored plastic "Shirley Temple" brooch

Printed cotton shirt has corduroy collar and white plastic buttons

Doll is dressed as fictional character Rebecca of Sunnybrook Farm

Separate fingers on left hand

Blue cotton knee-length trousers

Corduroy cuffs on rolled-up trousers

Knitted cotton knee-length socks

Black plastic slip-on shoes

SHIRLEY TEMPLE *The Ideal Novelty and Toy Company first issued Shirley Temple dolls in the 1930s, when little Shirley was the number one box office attraction in the United States. This 1960s hard vinyl version is modeled on the heroine of the film Rebecca of Sunnybrook Farm, in which Shirley Temple starred in 1938.*

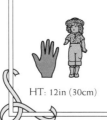

HT: 12in (30cm)

Original packaging, with clear plastic film front and Ideal logo

Rooted nylon hair, styled into ringlets

1930s SHIRLEY TEMPLE (RIGHT) One of the original Shirley Temple models, this doll was designed by Bernard Lipfert. Side-glancing eyes and a head of golden "Shirley Temple" curls give it an irresistible appeal. From 1934 to 1938, more than six million dolls of this popular young actress were sold. Ht: 25½in (64cm)

Flirty, sleeping eyes move from side to side and open and close

Composition reverse socket head

Bent composition arms

Cotton shoes conceal straight composition legs

1982 SHIRLEY TEMPLE (ABOVE) Ideal marketed this updated Shirley Temple in its Classic Doll line. The head is made of soft vinyl, with a hard vinyl body that looks much the same as the 1960s model. The clothing is cotton, with cloth lace-up shoes. Ht: 8½in (22cm)

© IDEAL 1982 HONG KONG

The copyright mark indicates that the doll was made in Hong Kong for Ideal in 1982.

CAMPBELL KID (BELOW) Designed by E.I. Horsman in 1910, this composition doll was one of a line used to advertise Campbell's Soup. Horsman went on to produce a number of unusual character dolls in plastic. Ht: 12in (30cm)

Painted facial features

ANNE SHIRLEY (BELOW) Effanbee (the trademark of Fleischaker and Baum, in New York) drew on L.M. Montgomery's novel Anne of Green Gables to create its all-composition Anne Shirley in 1936. The high quality of Effanbee's composition dolls was maintained in later plastic models. Ht: 15in (38cm)

Human hair wig, a replacement dating from the early 1960s

Molded hair, with baby curls

Composition flange neck head

Composition arms are jointed at shoulders

Chest label advertises Campbell's Soup

Sleeping eyes

Composition arms are jointed at shoulders

Bent composition limbs

Overalls conceal composition legs, jointed at hips

Doll wears lacy knit coat over long knitted dress and bootees

Flat feet are painted to resemble shoes and socks

1924 GRUMPY (LEFT) This cloth and composition doll from Effanbee was first issued in 1914. Grumpy dolls proved very popular, and many companies included one among their products. Ht: 14½in (36.5cm)

Smock conceals all-composition construction

Cotton smock with heart motif

The Changing Face of Barbie

· 1959 to the present day ·

LEGENDARY "TEEN-AGE FASHION MODEL" BARBIE is probably one of the best known of all modern dolls. Inspired by the risqué Lilli – a mid-1950s cartoon character in the German newspaper *Bild-Zeitung* – Barbie was developed by California-based Mattel, Inc., from one of the original Lilli dolls. The first Barbie was issued in 1959 and represented a stylized adult female. The doll had an elegant, slim waist, high, shapely breasts, and long, slender limbs; her facial features were exaggerated with heavy make-up. The clothing followed the most fashionable styles of the day and seemed to be fantasy – or at least idealized – creations.

Since the 1960s, Barbie's facial features have been greatly modified. Models from the 1980s and 1990s have a natural, youthful appearance, with smiling mouths and wide eyes. Their clothes and accessories are designed to reflect changing lifestyles.

Simulated mother-of-pearl hair decoration

Nylon (saran) hair is rooted into the head

Reverse socket head, made of soft vinyl

Open/closed, slightly thin-lipped mouth is fixed into a broad smile

Wide-staring eyes, painted turquoise and black

Hard vinyl arms are bent at elbows

Shoulder joints allow circular, horizontal, and vertical movement

Plastic "diamond" jewelry

Hip-length bodice in stretch nylon

Hard plastic body

Sumptuous ball gown has layers of vibrant pink-and-silver net over a pink nylon underskirt

Rigid legs, jointed only at hips

Swivel waist enables the torso to turn a full 360°

Feet are molded into standing-on-toes position

Flexible toes

"HAPPY HOLIDAYS" BARBIE

A standard model, made in China, this Special Edition 1990 Barbie comes with a signed photograph. It has numerous outfits and can also wear those of similar-sized dolls.

HT: 12in (30cm)

DOLL MARKS

The Mattel, Inc., mark and copyright date are pressed into the back of the head.

The body mark appears at the back of the torso on the waist or right buttock.

The Barbie logo is distinctive and has changed little over the years.

Barbie®

1950s LILLI (ABOVE) The original Lilli dolls were vampish, reflecting the exploits of the cartoon character. This German model is made of hard vinyl, with a reverse socket head. Ht: 12in (30cm)

Arched eyebrows

Flirtatious, side-glancing eyes, with molded eyelashes

Pert mouth

1962 "BUBBLE-CUT BARBIE" (ABOVE) With her short hairdo — new in 1962 — "Bubble-cut Barbie" has all the sophistication, but none of the toughness, of the Lilli dolls. Ht: 12in (30cm)

Pouting red lips, drawn into a slight smile

1991 FULL-OF-LIFE BARBIE (ABOVE) Registered in 1990, this model glows with youth and vitality. The doll has a lean body and wears bright, wash'n'wear clothes from the "Ski Fun" set. Ht: 12in (30cm)

Painted eyes look straight ahead

BARBIE'S FERRARI (RIGHT) This doll-sized car, made in Italy in 1990 for Mattel, is a scale-model version of a Pininfarina 328 GTS. Inside, a 1990 Barbie wears an outfit from the "Springtime Fashions" set.

"Chrome" hubcaps, with Ferrari horse logo

Authentic styling details include rearview wing mirrors and snap-in seat belts

Soft polyethylene head, with rooted nylon hair

Outfit is a perfect replica of the official American Airlines uniform

Catalog contains outfits for Barbie, boyfriend Ken, and best friend Midge

Original 1950s Mattel, Inc., logo

Emergency phone numbers

"AMERICAN AIRLINES STEWARDESS" (RIGHT) Clothes transform the basic Barbie into myriad roles. This set was made c.1963, and is modeled here by one of the earliest dolls. Ht: 12in (30cm)

Miniature regulation flight bag has a working zipper

Regulation black shoulder bag

School books with carrying strap

BABY-SITTER KIT (LEFT) The "Barbie baby-sits!" set, just one of Barbie's many accessories, was introduced in 1962, and came complete with a pair of reading glasses, a telephone for essential calls, and pretzels to munch.

Sandals replace original classic high-heel pumps

English Manufacturers

· 1950s to 1980s ·

ENGLISH DOLL-MAKING thrived in the middle years of the twentieth century. A number of firms that had begun production in the 1920s and 1930s coped admirably with the new developments in manufacturing techniques and materials, created their own distinctive style and designs, and were often very successful. ~ By the mid-1980s, however, financial difficulties had driven many companies out of business altogether. Others had become absorbed by larger international corporations, which moved the manufacturing of their dolls to other countries, especially those in eastern Asia, where labor was cheaper and production costs were lower. The dolls on these pages were made by some of the most prestigious firms of the 1950s to the 1980s.

Printed card in metal ring, attached to the doll's wrist by a string.

Long, rooted nylon hair can be brushed into bangs

Doll wears a good-quality cotton gingham dress over white cotton underpants

Socket head can turn

Stylized facial features

Painted brown eyes, with painted black upper lashes and a tinge of blue eyeshadow above

Hard vinyl body is jointed at shoulders

Torso is made in two parts but does not turn

Molded hands, with joined fingers and separate thumbs

Joints at hips allow movement of legs

Wrist tag is the doll's only marking

Straight legs, with rounded calves

Flat feet, with no instep, enable the doll to stand unaided

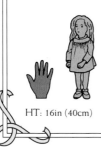

TRENDON, SASHA DOLL *Sasha Morgenthaler of Zurich, Switzerland, designed the Sasha line of hard vinyl dolls, first produced by Trendon Ltd. of Stockport, Cheshire, UK, in 1965. Girls, boys, and babies were available in three colorings: the flesh tone varied, depending on whether the doll had blond, brunette, or black hair. This example is Sasha Brunette No. 103, issued in 1970.*

HT: 16in (40cm)

Leather shoes, with snap-fastening ankle straps

Prototype heads are made of plaster, painted in watercolors

Various hair colors are available

Daisy, with the original English-language packaging for a fashion outfit

Side-glancing eyes suggest a youthful girl, full of fun

Final chosen version of the Daisy head

DAISY PROTOTYPES (ABOVE) Mary Quant designed a number of different types of face for Daisy until she was satisfied that the features of the doll represented those of a typical English "model girl."

PEDIGREE, KELLY (RIGHT) Kelly, a fully poseable fashion doll, was designed by Bruce Beresford and produced by Pedigree Soft Toys Ltd. exclusively for a chain of retail stores in the United Kingdom. Kelly was briefly available at the end of 1979. Ht: 11in (28cm)

MARY QUANT'S DAISY (LEFT) The dress designer Mary Quant, working with Flair Toys, introduced Daisy in 1973, and it was produced for ten years. Although Mary Quant designed all of the clothing, much of it was manufactured in Hong Kong, along with the doll itself. Ht: 9in (23cm)

Socket head can turn

Chestnut brown, rooted saran hair

Mary Quant's trademark gives the doll its name

Sleeping blue plastic eyes, with nylon lashes

Painted closed mouth

Dress conceals soft vinyl body

Cotton dress designed by Hazel Smith

Straight legs are jointed at hips

White vinyl shoes, with button fastening

Rooted nylon hair

Painted facial features

Reverse socket head is made of soft vinyl

ROSEBUD (RIGHT) Eric and Hazel Smith of Northampton registered the name Rosebud as a trademark for a line of dolls in 1947. This model, manufactured in 1963, has a pretty dolly face. Ht: 18½in (47cm)

Molded and painted hair

Inset eyes, without lashes

Body is jointed at shoulders

Bent limbs

Joints at hips allow legs to move

All-plastic, injection-molded body

RODDY DOLL (LEFT) Using a combination of their names, doll-makers D.G. Todd and J. Robinson created a line of dolls called Roddy in the late 1930s. This typical injection-molded baby doll was manufactured c.1955. Ht: 12in (30cm)

Buttoned armchair is made of vinyl

Sindy and Patch

· 1960s to the present day ·

A FASHION DOLL with a youthful image, Sindy was designed by Dennis Arkinstall and first issued by the Pedigree Doll Company of Canterbury, Kent, England, in 1962. Marketed as "the doll you love to dress," Sindy was available with a wide range of different outfits and accessories that reflected the changing styles of the time. The doll soon had family and friends, including Patch, the younger sister, and Paul, the boyfriend (see page 127).

～ Sindy was remodeled in 1971 and given a more shapely, elegant form to keep up with fashion trends. Then, in 1987, when Pedigree went out of business, Hasbro in the United States bought the doll. Sindy has since been redesigned and now has an active, sporty image to suit current fashions.

Long, rooted nylon hair can be combed and even styled with rollers

Retroussé nose

Closed mouth is painted red

Plastic diamanté choker fits closely around neck

Evening gloves stretch to above elbow height

Reverse socket head is made of soft vinyl

Painted side-glancing eyes, with painted lashes

Hard plastic body is jointed at shoulders

Within the limbs, a special inner framework permits the elbows, knees, and ankles to be posed

Hands have long, thin, separately molded fingers

Long, shapely soft vinyl legs are jointed at hips

Swivel waist allows the torso to turn a full 360°

Mold lines are visible down center of legs

Stylish evening dress, with ruched and gathered sides

Elegant matching evening bag, with "gold" chain

Feet are shaped to fit into high-heeled shoes

Green plastic slip-on high heels

1971 SINDY *The "second-generation" Sindy boasted a completely new body, created by Ian Daniels. It has a special framework inside the vinyl "skin," which allows the elbows, knees, and ankles to move freely or to lock in one position. At this time, Sindy's wardrobe offered many different accessories and outfits, including this glamorous evening dress.*

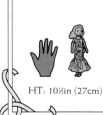

HT: 10½in (27cm)

Annotations for 1962 Sindy (left doll):
- Rooted curled blond hair of coarse nylon
- Soft vinyl head
- Painted features
- Clothes conceal hard vinyl body and soft vinyl limbs
- Beneath sweater, lower torso carries raised mark "MADE IN HONG KONG"

Annotations for 1990s "Top Model" Sindy:
- Platinum blond nylon hair
- Soft vinyl reverse socket head, with painted facial features
- Within the limbs, internal joints allow the elbows and knees to bend
- Costume conceals hard vinyl body, jointed at hips and shoulders

DOLL MARKS

The logo on the packaging reflects changing styles.

The first Sindy signature was in a simple script, suggesting a youthful hand.

The 1990s signature is more stylish, and often in two colors instead of one.

1962 SINDY (LEFT)
Dressed in clothes typical of the early 1960s, this was the first Sindy model in the line. The body has a more girlish form than that of the doll that followed, and the feet are flat. Ht: 12in (30cm)

1990s "TOP MODEL" SINDY (LEFT)
Reissued by Hasbro, modern-day Sindy has a sporty look and a wide, confident smile. This example has encased joints at the elbows and knees. Ht: 11in (28cm)

"FUN BIKE" SINDY (BELOW)
Reflecting a newfound passion for cycling among children and fitness fanatics of all ages, in 1990 Hasbro produced a Sindy model with "pedal power action" and, of course, her very own mountain bike. Ht: 10½in (27cm)

Annotations for "Fun Bike" Sindy:
- Cyclist's helmet, echoing current concerns about safety
- Soft vinyl head
- Clothes conceal hard vinyl body, jointed at shoulders and hips
- Open joints at knees allow legs to bend and stretch
- Bike is in working order: wheels, pedals, and legs move together
- Dazzling fluorescent colors, fashionable in the early 1990s
- Bicycle is 12in (30cm) long

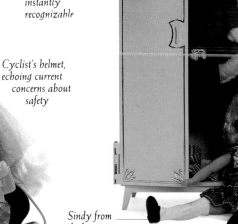

- The insignia of the letter "S" enclosed in a heart shape makes Sindy accessories instantly recognizable
- Sindy from the late 1960s

SINDY'S WARDROBE (ABOVE)
Among the many accessories for Sindy are a wardrobe, a house, and a car. Dolls with complete sets of clothing and accessories have been popular for many years.

"TOBOGGAN TIME" PATCH
(BELOW) Issued as Sindy's younger sister in 1966, Patch is shorter than Sindy and, because of her youth, has a less well-developed body and a flatter chest than her sister Ht: 23cm (9in)

Annotations for "Toboggan Time" Patch:
- Rooted short nylon hair
- Painted features, with freckles
- Hard plastic toboggan
- Clothes conceal soft vinyl limbs and hard vinyl torso

Baby and Toddler Dolls

· 1940s to the present day ·

ENCOURAGED BY ADVANCES in equipment and technology in the 1930s, manufacturers of baby dolls began to produce models that were ever more realistic. Those that "performed" in some way – feeding, wetting, or crying – proved to be long-term favorites. In recent years, designers have even created dolls that look as if they have diaper rash, and those that will "eat" solid food. With the aid of batteries, some dolls will laugh, crawl, and even repeat words that are spoken to them.

Many models portray newborn babies, and some are available complete with hospital ID bracelets and navel bindings, as well as birth certificates. Some dolls are anatomically correct, made either as boys or as girls. But these have proved controversial, being considered by some people to carry realism too far.

Manufacturer's trademark is molded into upper back of the torso.

Molded hair

Flange neck head is turned to one side

Soft vinyl construction, jointed at shoulders and hips

Molded Effe logo on back of doll

Bent limbs

Flat feet with spread toes are typical of a newborn baby's

Hands are molded in characteristic baby pose

Navel bandage provides authentic detail

Inset plastic eyes; baby dolls usually have sleeping eyes

Open/closed mouth

Wrist band carries label printed with name, imitating hospital ID bracelet

Slightly "baggy" flesh, with folds, wrinkles, and creases

Realistically styled male genitalia

Hands are molded to show typical baby dimples

BIMBOVERO EFFE *Designed in Italy mainly for the English and American markets, this 1980s baby doll was available either as a girl or as a boy. The whole doll is made of soft vinyl and molded so that the flesh resembles that of a newborn baby, with wrinkles, dimples, and skin folds. The doll has a built-in scent of talcum powder and baby lotion.*

HT: 17½in (45cm)

Cardboard cradle forms part of the doll's packaging

Open mouth, with toothless gums

Rooted blond nylon hair

Pert expression changes when doll's torso is squeezed

Name of doll is printed on the side of the cradle

Dress covers abdomen containing voice box

FIRST LOVE (ABOVE)

A newborn baby girl doll, First Love was marketed in the 1980s by the English Pedigree Doll Company, although it was actually manufactured by Berjusa of Spain. The doll is made of soft vinyl and smells of baby lotion. Ht: 15in (35cm)

Side glancing painted blue eyes, with painted lashes

MOVING MOUTH BABY

(LEFT and ABOVE) Squeezing the abdomen of this baby doll makes its mouth open and close, and elicits a squeak. Manufactured in Hong Kong and copyrighted by Mattel in the United States in 1966, the doll is made of vinyl, and jointed at the shoulders and hips. Ht: 7in (18cm)

Dress conceals all-composition body, jointed at shoulders and hips

Spotted cotton dress and bonnet, over white petticoat and flannelette diaper

Pink shoes, with lace trim, match the dress and pants

Bent limbs

Decorative red ribbons are sewn onto dress and bonnet

SUNSHINE BABY (LEFT)

One of Vogue Dolls' classic baby models, the Sunshine Baby is an all-composition doll, which was produced in the 1940s. Its name reflects the optimism prevalent in the United States during the post-war years. Ht: 8in (20cm)

"POTTY TIME" QUINTS

(BELOW) The "Drink and Wet" set is just one in the Quints line copyrighted in 1991 by Tyco Industries, Inc., of New Jersey and made in China. Each of these tiny toddler dolls has a pair of pants and a baby bottle, and they come with a bench that contains five heart-shaped potties. Ht: 2½in (6cm)

Blond hair is tied up in a ponytail with ribbon

Curly rooted saran hair

Reverse socket head

Soft vinyl construction, jointed at shoulders and hips

Open mouth for bottle

Color-coordinated pants match the potty seats

Each of the five potty seats is identified with a color and number

Hole at bottom of torso for liquid to come out

Plastic baby bottles can be filled with water

123

Royal Doulton and Nisbet

· 1980 to 1985 ·

IN THE FIRST HALF of the 1980s, two English firms joined forces to manufacture several series of collectors' dolls: Royal Doulton, a porcelain company renowned for its figurines and table china; and the House of Nisbet, already well known for its costume dolls. The dolls' porcelain heads and lower arms were created by Eric Griffiths, who had formerly worked for the famous Pedigree Doll Company. Alison Nisbet – daughter of Nisbet's founder, Peggy – designed their stuffed calico bodies and clothing. Most of the series were issued in editions limited to 3,000 or 5,000. Each doll was individually boxed and came with a certificate bearing the limited edition number. Production ceased in 1985.

Well-modeled porcelain shoulder head

Painted facial features

Shoulder head is sewn to body through holes in front and back of shoulder plate

Stuffed calico upper arms and torso, with disk joints at the shoulders

Porcelain lower arms, with hands molded into an expressive gesture

Stuffed calico legs are stitched to torso at hips

Seams at tops of thighs allow doll to sit

Crudely shaped feet, with no toes

Real feathers decorate the hat

Soft brown velvet hat

Long curled mohair wig

Luxuriant feel and appearance of the fabrics complement the fine quality and modeling of the porcelain head and lower arms

Wrist tag announces the Royal Doulton/ Nisbet partnership, as well as the name of the doll

Velvet muff is attached to one wrist

Royal Doulton NISBET WINTER

Textured satin dress is trimmed with crushed velvet at neck, wrist, and hem

WINTER *Drawings by the artist Kate Greenaway inspired a series of Collectors' Dolls, issued in 1981, whose elegant period costumes have a seasonal theme. In this example, the doll is dressed in deep, rich red and brown – colors traditionally associated with winter. The lavish velvet trimmings generate a sense of genuine warmth and comfort.*

HT: 10½in (27cm)

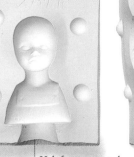

THREE-PIECE HEAD MOLD

(LEFT) The plaster mold for the porcelain head is in three parts, held together by thick elastic bands. Bone china slip is poured into the hole at the top and, when it has hardened, the casts are removed. Called "blue heads" because of their color at this stage, they need to be smoothed down before firing.

Side of shoulder plate — Hole for pouring in bone china slip

DOLL MARKS

Every doll bears the Royal Doulton copyright mark on the shoulder plate.

~

Special collections have their own individual copyright mark.

D.N 19
© ROYAL DOULTON
TABLEWARE LTD. 1981
KATE GREENAWAY
DOLL COLLECTION

Limited-edition dolls come with a certificate of authentication.

Royal Doulton
NISBET

FACE PAINTING

(RIGHT) After the heads are smoothed and fired, they are given either a pink or an ivory matte glaze. Then the facial features are painted and fired several times to set each color. The outline of the eyes and lashes come first, then the irises and pupils. Adding blush pink color to the lips and cheeks gives the finishing touch. Head ht: 2⅓in (6cm)

Collectors' series doll heads are all identical

Eye color changes according to model of doll

Feather duster, made of real feathers

SATURDAY GIRL (LEFT)

"Saturday's child works hard for a living," from the children's birthday rhyme, provides the theme for one of the first dolls produced under the Royal Doulton/Nisbet name. Ht: 10½in (27cm)

Shoulder-length blond mohair wig

Doll wears a maid's uniform

Stuffed calico hands, with the fingers indicated only by stitches; later models have porcelain hands

Cardboard label hanging from wrist identifies the doll and the series to which it belongs

Flange neck head

Painted hair and features

Full, pouting lips give the doll a distinguished mouth

Plastic socket joints at shoulders and hips allow the limbs to move freely

Porcelain lower arms

Porcelain lower legs to above knees

Porcelain lower legs

FIRSTBORN (ABOVE)

The baby doll of the Royal Doulton/ Nisbet series was issued in 1982. Its dumpy calico body is rather out of keeping with the well-cast porcelain head and lower limbs, but the doll's charm lies in its appearance when clothed. Ht: 12in (30cm)

Men and Boys
· 1960s to the present day ·

THE NUMBER OF MALE DOLLS has always tended to be small compared to the number of females, reflecting the industry's belief that boys do not play with dolls. More male models are being produced, as it becomes clear that children of both sexes like to play with dolls of all kinds. The best-known male doll is G.I. Joe, or Action Man as it was named in the United Kingdom, first issued in 1964. G.I. Joe was inescapably macho, and very much a military man. As antiwar feelings grew in the late 1960s, so G.I. Joe's popularity waned, and the doll was re-marketed in the form of a "global adventurer." Production ceased in the 1980s, but in 1993 Hasbro, the copyright-holder, launched the doll with new and updated accessories.

Raised, molded mark on torso indicates manufacturer and copyright-holder.

Waterproof suit made of unbleached calico

Molded hair; later models have flock hair

Painted eyes and eyebrows

Molded and painted scar on cheek

Soft vinyl socket head turns a full 360°

Diving belt has metal weights

Torso is fully formed, with well-molded pectoral muscles

Identity tag bears Action Man logo

Jointing at waist allows torso to swivel 360°

Waterproof calico mittens, elasticized at the wrist

Well-modeled hands, showing knuckles and fingernails, are specially designed to grip "equipment"

Hard vinyl body, with ball and socket joints at hips and waist

Waterproof calico mittens, elasticized at the wrist

Hinged ball and socket joints at knees, elbows, shoulders, wrists, and ankles allow them to move freely

Shapely legs have distinctive calf muscles, with visible tendons

Plastic sheath knife is strapped to the calf with elastic

Long, arched feet have well-shaped toes with toenails

Plastic helmet finished to look like brass; air hose attaches to the back

Plastic boots, with metallic weighted clogs

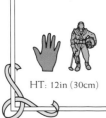

1964 ACTION MAN Described as "The movable fighting man," the first Action Man has 20 moving parts and can be posed to run, kneel, sit, crawl, stand, or lie flat. When immersed in water, the deep-sea diver set shown here creates surprisingly realistic underwater effects.

HT: 12in (30cm)

The "Official Action Soldier," dressed in U.S. Army regulation denims

G.I. JOE'S SCOUT CAR
(BELOW) All kinds of toy military vehicles have been produced for G.I. Joe, and models have been updated in keeping with actual changes taking place in the armed forces.

Molded and painted hair

Felt cowboy hat

Wrist tag reads "Hi! I'm Jimmy"

Metal toy gun on wrist ribbon

Blue cotton dungarees conceal soft vinyl body, with dimpled limbs

Scout car based on World War II models

VOGUE'S JIMMY (ABOVE) Dressed as a small boy playing cowboy, Jimmy was issued by Vogue Dolls, Inc., in the 1960s. The soft vinyl doll is similar to those in Vogue's Ginnette series (see page 113). Ht: 8in (20cm)

MATTEL'S 1961 KEN (BELOW)
The advertising slogan "He's a doll" introduced Ken, Barbie's boyfriend (see page 116), in 1961. The first model had a semihard vinyl head and hard vinyl body. The doll's expression and slender physique suggest a clean-living, shy young man. Ht: 12in (30cm)

Luxuriant, rooted nylon hair

Shirt conceals bent arms, with modified ball joints at shoulders

Torso pivots slightly at the waist

Set includes hair gel, booklet with styling tips, and five hair accessories

Molded and painted hair

Movable head

Painted green eyes

Blond flock "crew-cut" hair

Painted eyes, with molded lids and lashes

Suit conceals straight, unjointed arms and legs

Small hands, with indented fingernails

Simple packaging, printed in one language

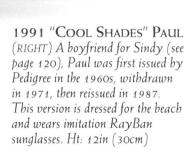

1991 "ULTRA HAIR" KEN
(ABOVE) As with Barbie, Mattel has made major alterations to Ken, to keep pace with changing trends. This model has the well-muscled body of an athletic young man, and hair that can be coiffed with styling gel. Ht: 12in (30cm)

Sophisticated packaging, printed in several languages

1991 "COOL SHADES" PAUL
(RIGHT) A boyfriend for Sindy (see page 120), Paul was first issued by Pedigree in the 1960s, withdrawn in 1971, then reissued in 1987. This version is dressed for the beach and wears imitation RayBan sunglasses. Ht: 12in (30cm)

Doll's name is printed on T-shirt

Hard vinyl limbs, tinted to give the doll a suntanned appearance

New Doll Ideas

· 1960s to the present day ·

THE BOOM YEARS of the twentieth century saw a change of pace in the doll world. Although the traditional models were as popular as ever, novelty dolls came and went as styles changed. Some reflected the political atmosphere of the time, such as the movement against nuclear weapons, the anarchy of punk rock – or the renewed emphasis on the importance of the family unit. The versatility of plastic, combined with the ingenuity of the manufacturers, allowed ever more complex designs.

Not all modern dolls are plastic. Michael and Lynne Roche of Bath, England, are among a number of individual makers who have returned to using mainly natural materials for their dolls. Beth, one of their designs, shows the best of English doll-making in the 1990s.

The maker's mark appears beneath the hairline on the back of the head.

Initials of Lynne Roche and date of manufacture appear below left ear.

Red-blond mohair wig

Well-shaped bisque socket head

Painted mouth

Inset blue glass eyes

Yellow knitted cardigan has colored wooden buttons

Traditionally shaped wooden body

Ball joints at the elbows, shoulders, and wrists

Bisque hands are large and expressive

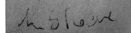

Signature of Michael Roche, maker of the body, inscribed on the right buttock.

Ball joints at hips allow doll to sit

Ball joints at knees allow flexibility

Calves are smooth and well carved

Cat-shaped toy, made of printed cotton, fits snugly into back pocket of doll's dungarees

Flat feet are carved to show toes

Blue denim dungarees are fastened at front with wooden buttons

BISQUE AND WOODEN DOLL, BETH *Created by Michael and Lynne Roche in Bath, England, in 1992, Beth embodies the 1990s revival of interest in traditional crafts and the use of natural materials. The doll has a turned wooden body and finely cast bisque head and hands. Its clothing is also made from natural fibers: wool and cotton, with leather for the shoes.*

HT: 11in (28cm)

Red leather shoes, with button fastening

JUDITH "MOTHER AND BABY" (RIGHT)

This innovative – if unrealistic – "pregnant" doll, issued in 1992, was designed by Villy Nielsen A/S in Denmark and manufactured by the Lucky Bell Plastics Company in Hong Kong. Ht: 11in (28cm)

1985 PUNK ROCKER

(LEFT) A representative of the punk scene that began in the mid-1970s, this hard vinyl doll is one of a pair issued by Marian Kenny Designs in England. Ht: 7½in (19cm)

FATHER
Ht: 12in (30cm)

Soft vinyl head, with molded hair and painted features

Shirt conceals hard vinyl body, jointed at shoulders and hips

Clothes for boy twin coordinate with those for father

Soft vinyl head

Large, rounded tummy lifts off to allow baby to be removed. Then spring-loaded flat tummy moves into place

Loose-fitting cotton and polyester clothing conceals hard vinyl body

Molded sandals, with painted details

Maternity clothes, as well as accessories for the baby, are available

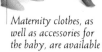
BOY TWIN
Ht: 4in (10cm)

C.N.D. MARCHERS (ABOVE)

The rise of the peace movement in the 1950s and 1960s inspired the design of these two supporters of the British Campaign for Nuclear Disarmament. Manufactured in hard vinyl, the dolls are dressed in beatnik style and wear C.N.D. medallions. Ht: 7½in (19cm)

MOTHER
Ht: 12in (30cm)

THE HEART FAMILY (BELOW) Mattel,

in the United States, created its own nuclear family in 1985, when it packaged two adult dolls together with twin baby dolls. In the six years the Hearts were in production, the line grew to include grandparents, baby cousins, and neighborhood kids.

Vinyl accessories include highchair, baby bath, and pony rocker

Hard vinyl baby doll, with bent limbs
GIRL TWIN
Ht: 4in (10cm)

Mother's outfit matches that of little girl

National Dolls

National dolls take many forms, ranging from folk-art dolls crafted by indigenous peoples to record their culture, and patriotic dolls that celebrate popular heroes or historic events, to souvenir dolls in national costumes, which are not always made in the country they are intended to represent. In some cases the designs or materials used have changed over the years, but many national dolls are still made in accordance with centuries-old traditions.

THE NOTION OF NATIONAL DOLLS developed in the eighteenth century, as many more Europeans ventured abroad. People collected dolls as mementos of their travels. In some countries, no tradition of national dolls existed. Europeans introduced the concept, with the aim of recording the different ways of life and costumes in these places – sometimes with commercial advantages for the Europeans themselves.

Dolls in China and Japan

The best known of the national dolls are the Japanese festival dolls. For more than 400 years, these figures have been used for very specific purposes. Boys are taught the virtues of manliness, loyalty, and chivalry; and girls are trained to understand the duties and virtues of being a good wife and mother. The children also learn of their nation's history and culture through this process. These dolls are put on display only once a year, on the appropriate festival day – March 3 for girls, and May 5 for boys (see pages 132–133).

⌒ At *Tango no sekku*, the Boys' Festival, the doll display is set out on a two- or three-tiered stand.

Dolls representing samurai warriors and legendary characters are featured, as well as miniature models of swords, banners, hats, and horses. *Ohina matsuri*, the Girls' Festival, is more complex. As a mother and daughter set out the dolls on a five- or seven-tiered stand, the mother explains the significance of each of the figures. Models of the Emperor and Empress, court officials, and musicians and servants are included among the dolls. Miniature household furnishings are also shown, and are placed on the lower tiers. Various personal objects that represent the dowry of a bride from a noble or samurai family, and offerings of rice cakes and sake, are also displayed on the lower tiers.

⌒ Over the years, the dolls have changed hardly at all. The makers stay faithful to the traditional styles with as much accuracy as is possible, and do not try to develop or improve on the designs.

⌒ *Kokeshi* are another, entirely different, kind of traditional Japanese doll.

SOUTH AFRICAN MISSION DOLL (LEFT) *This stuffed felt doll and its intricately beaded costume were made in a Red Cross Rehabilitation Center in Durban, c.1960. Dolls like this were sold to raise money in support of the center. Ht: 13in (33cm)*

MEXICAN PAPIER-MACHE DANCER (RIGHT) *A traditional design of brightly painted papier-mâché was the inspiration for this Mexican doll, which was made in 1991. It is a folk-art doll and is rather crude, but colorful. The doll's arms and legs are jointed with elastic. Ht: 13in (33cm)*

KOKESHI CRAFTSMAN IN JAPAN (LEFT) *Each maker of the turned wooden kokeshi may give his dolls a slightly different shape and paint them in his own special signature design. Whole "families" of these traditional kokeshi are made, in a wide range of sizes.*

NEW ORLEANS SUGAR-CANE CUTTER (RIGHT) *This wax figure is one of a series of dolls that portray the traditional trades of the state of Louisiana. It was made by a member of the Vargas family, sometime between 1915 and the 1930s. Ht: 7in (18cm)*

They have been made in the northeastern region of Japan since the early seventeenth century. *Kokeshi* are fashioned from turned wood and given a decorative painted finish. These dolls are limbless, having only a head and a body. Originally designed as religious symbols, *kokeshi* became toys for children; nowadays they are sold mainly as souvenirs.

In China, children played not with dolls, but with small, brightly colored clay figures, often representing animals. Dolls in the Western style were introduced by Europeans to help to preserve a record of the way of life in China. Many dolls such as these were made at missions that had been set up toward the end of the nineteenth century to aid children in need. Found mainly in the southern provinces of Kiangsu, Fukien, and Chekiang, carved wooden dolls, such as those from the Door of Hope Missions (see pages 134–135), were dressed by the children and sold to raise funds for the missions themselves. Dolls were also sold as souvenirs in the markets and bazaars of China. These were made out of wire and clay, or painted plaster, and represented theatrical dancers and performers.

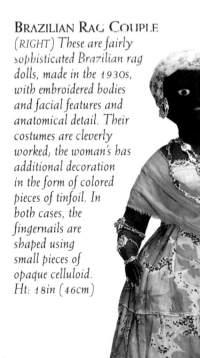

BRAZILIAN RAG COUPLE (RIGHT) *These are fairly sophisticated Brazilian rag dolls, made in the 1930s, with embroidered bodies and facial features and anatomical detail. Their costumes are cleverly worked; the woman's has additional decoration in the form of colored pieces of tinfoil. In both cases, the fingernails are shaped using small pieces of opaque celluloid. Ht: 18in (46cm)*

Dolls of Russia

The *matryoshka*, or nesting dolls, have long been associated with Russia (see pages 136–137), although the idea for dolls that fit inside each other probably comes from China. Various styles of doll were traditionally made in Russia, as in other eastern European countries, to record the peoples, costumes, and culture of the different regions; today they are produced primarily as souvenirs to sell to tourists. Customarily, wood was used to make these dolls, but in recent years, rag has often been used.

National dolls, especially the folk-art kind, are always popular with foreign visitors, but they have a value far greater than mere souvenirs. They provide paid employment for the makers, help to record the customs and traditions of the country, and preserve the craft of doll-making itself.

Japanese Dolls

· 1900s to 1960s ·

MANY JAPANESE DOLLS are designed not as playthings but as ornaments, often depicting some aspect of Japanese history or culture. The intriguing *sakura-ningyō* (cherry dolls) may be modeled on Kabuki dancers, or they may portray some aspect of everyday life. It has long been a favorite pastime among young women to make and dress these figures. Today, cherry dolls are also produced commercially, mainly for export or as souvenirs, but they are still popular display items in Japanese homes. ⁓ Dolls in the decorative category known as *hina-ningyo* (festival dolls) serve a second purpose. Brought out only on the children's festival days each year, these dolls, which are handed down from generation to generation, are used to illustrate the traditions of the nation.

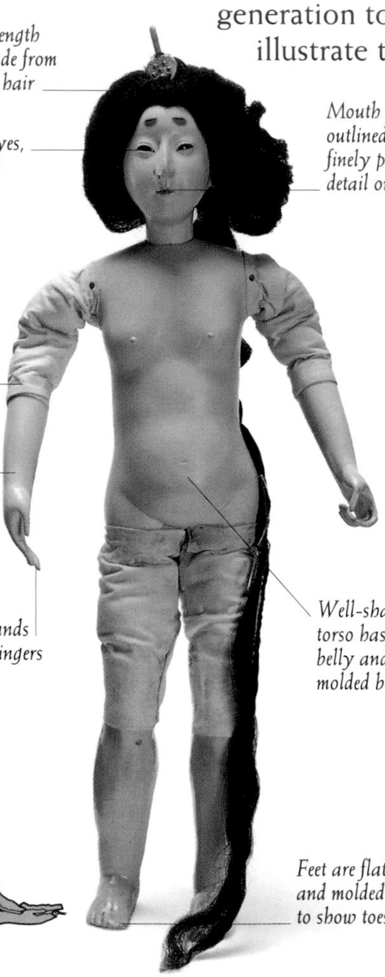

Gilt metal comb
adorns the hair

Gofun-covered
socket head

Floor-length
wig made from
human hair

Inset glass eyes,
with painted
eyebrows

Mouth is
outlined, with
finely painted
detail on lips

Wooden fan, with
painted decoration

Cloth upper
arms and thighs

Green silk
kimono over
white damask
kimono

Composition
lower limbs and
torso, painted to
match coloring
of the head

Stylized hands
with long fingers

Well-shaped
torso has rounded
belly and
molded breasts

Feet are flat
and molded
to show toes

Long
silk crepe
trousers

HT: 13in (33cm)

CEREMONIAL FIGURE WITH FAN *Representing the wife of a high-ranking official of the court, this majestic figure in ceremonial robes dates from the early 20th century. The doll has an unusually extensive wardrobe of elaborate costumes, which are made of silk and damask.*

Plaster composition
head and hands

MOUNTED WARRIOR
(LEFT) An important element of
Tango-no-sekku, the Boys'
Festival, this ornate figure is
part of the set that conveys
the code of the samurai,
Japan's aristocratic
warrior class. Ht:
10in (25cm)

SHOKI, THE DEVIL CHASER
(RIGHT) By tradition, Japanese
families displayed an image of a
legendary character, Shoki, at
the Boys' Festival in the belief
that he would protect their sons
from evil. This figure is a late 19th-
century doll, designed to hold only
one pose. Ht: 22in (55cm)

Horse is made
of a padded
wire armature
covered with
animal
skin

Silk brocade
costume, with
gold-painted
paper armor

Padded costume is part
of construction of doll
and cannot be removed

Elaborate robes
made of padded
silk brocade

Ornaments
are carved
from wood,
then gilded

CEREMONIAL PAIR (BELOW)
The figure on the left of this boxed
set is described in detail opposite.
The other doll represents a man,
ready to be dressed as a top-level
official of the emperor's court.

Carved and
lacquered
wooden stand

Gofun-covered
lower limbs
and torso

Patterned silk
kimono, with
long sleeves

Stand is made
of lacquered and
painted wood

Gilded
wooden
feet

Man's face
is natural
color; high-
ranking lady's
face is white

Bottom layer of
three-tiered black
lacquered
presentation
box; other layers
hold clothes and
accessories (see
page 149)

Feet bear
toed socks

SILENT ENVOY (ABOVE) Yamato-
ningyō, dolls representing children in
traditional dress, were originally designed
as gifts for royalty to present to honored
guests. More recently, such dolls have
been sent as "envoys of friendship" to
other countries. Ht: 13in (33cm)

Hair is a
silk wig

Face mask is
made of painted,
stiffened fabric

Male figure dressed
in silk undergarment;
ceremonial robes are
included in the set

MAIDEN WITH HATS (RIGHT)
This sakura-ningyō, or cherry
doll, portrays a Kabuki character
performing the "Dance of the
Seven Hats," an interpretation of
a Japanese folktale. The doll is
commercially made and dates from
the 1950s. Ht: 14in (35cm)

Hats are made of silk over
buckram, trimmed with gold

Fixed-pose body,
made of padded
cloth over a wire
armature

Doll is mounted
on a varnished
wooden stand

133

Chinese Dolls

· 1900s to 1950s ·

FROM THE EARLY NINETEENTH CENTURY to about 1950, almost all dolls and toys in mainland China were made in missions set up to help destitute children – often slaves, child widows, or prostitutes. Europeans were the driving force behind the missions and were hoping to retain the culture of the country while making attractive souvenirs that could be sold to raise funds for the missions' work.

Two important missions were based in Shanghai and Canton under the name Door of Hope. At the Shanghai center, which was opened in 1901, the girls were taught needlework, a skill they could use to dress wooden dolls, for which they were paid. The Canton mission made similar dolls using composition.

Painted eyes and hair

Heads are carved from pear or boxwood and polished smooth

Bright colors and decorative embroidery indicate child is of a higher social class than plainly uniformed nurse

Back of head is carved into a bun shape

Baby is 5½in (14cm) tall

Pink silk "sling" ties the baby to the nurse's back

Child's legs are made of stuffed cloth

Traditional suit of tunic over three-quarter-length trousers

Hands are carved from wood and then polished

Trousers conceal carved wooden legs

Front of costume has faded from exposure to sunlight

Fingers are fashioned together, but thumbs are separate

Clothing is made from scraps of fabric, donated by well-wishers

AMAH AND BABY Made at one of the Door of Hope missions between 1928 and 1930, these two dolls depict an amah – a child's nurse – carrying a baby on her back. In keeping with the custom for the working class at the time, the nurse's feet are not bound, although those of the baby's mother would be, since she is of a higher social status.

Shoes are black silk, with rolled tops and white soles

HT: 10½in (27cm)

MISSION DOLL FAMILY (BELOW)
This family of dolls from the 1930s is made of cotton and has embroidered features. The dolls' fingers are formed from loops of cotton. Ht: Largest 3in (7.5cm); smallest 2in (5cm)

The name SHAOHSING INDUSTRIAL MISSION, SHAOHSING, CHEKIANG PROVINCE, CHINA is printed at the top of the card

Molded and painted facial features

Female doll holds composition and cloth baby

Composition head and limbs; body is made of padded cloth over wire armature

Waistband has foil and paper decoration

Long silk dress, with three-quarter-length kimono

Silk costume is richly embroidered

FARMER AND WIFE (BELOW)
These dolls, dressed in the dark blue associated with the post war revolutionary period, are part of a set designed in the 1950s by Ada Lum. Their purpose was not only to provide a record of rural Chinese costumes, but also to give work to refugees who had fled to Hong Kong from mainland China in the wake of the revolution. Ht: 18in (46cm)

Woolen hair is braided into pigtail

Stuffed cotton head and body

Embroidered eyebrows and eyes

Lips are painted

PEKING OPERA CHARACTERS
(ABOVE) Two figures from a set made c.1900, these rare display dolls represent dancers of the Peking Opera. The man's high status is denoted by the elaborate embroidery on his silk costume. Ht: Woman 11in (28cm); man 11½in (29cm)

MANDARIN WITH LONG FINGERS (RIGHT)
Known to have been bought in Hong Kong c.1930, this doll may be one of those from the Door of Hope Mission at Canton. Similar dolls were adapted for use as puppets by attaching bamboo rods to their wrists. Ht: 10in (25cm)

Ornamental head-dress is made of stiffened, painted paper

Head and limbs made of painted composition over wood

Long fingers traditionally indicate that doll represents the aristocracy

Silk brocade costume, heavily ornamented and embroidered

Dolls are dressed in matching everyday outfits

Female has embroidered shoes of a type worn only indoors

Beach grass shoes for outdoor wear

Russian Dolls

· 1800s to the present day ·

TOYS, INCLUDING DOLLS, have been made in Russia and its neighboring republics for many centuries. In Russia, the tradition of making toys sprang from the monastery of Holy Trinity–St. Sergius (founded in 1337), where religious souvenirs were produced for pilgrims. The surrounding area, from Zagorsk (now called Sergiyev Posad) near Moscow to Bogorodskoye near Kirov, subsequently became the most important toy-producing region in the country.

The *matryoshka* or nesting dolls are possibly the best known of all Russian dolls. Made of turned, hollowed wood and painted in bright, vibrant colors, they decrease in size so that each fits inside the next largest. The groups usually vary in number between six and ten, but much larger sequences of 15 or more nesting dolls have also been produced.

Painted features and hair show regional characteristics

Figure is carved from a single piece of wood

Traditional costume of a lady's nursemaid

Widest side of triangle forms a flat back

Decoration is continued around the back of the figure

Small child at base of doll is carved from same piece of wood

Base shows original grain line

TRIANGULAR FIGURE *Wooden dolls of this type have been popular in Russia since the early 1800s. Most were made during the winter by peasants living in forest regions, for sale in town markets in spring. This late 19th-century example comes from Bogorodskoye and is one of a set representing wealthy provincial ladies and their nurse-maids. It is carved from one solid piece of wood and hand-painted.*

HT: 7in (18cm)

COZY RAG DOLL (BELOW)

From the 1930s to 1950s, many cloth dolls, in peasant or regional costume, were made as souvenirs. Variations on the theme abound: the padded-cloth skirt of this 1960s doll covers a samovar or teapot. The head is made of composition, as are the lower arms, on a stuffed cloth torso. Ht: 14in (35cm)

DOLLS FROM FOUR REPUBLICS (RIGHT)

All 1960s souvenirs, these figures represent four different republics. This kind of doll was usually made of molded, compressed paper, sometimes mixed with pulped rag, then painted. Ht: 3½in (9cm)

Solid, not hollow, construction

Tissue paper accessories

Varnish protects painted features and delicate skin tones

Thin paper hands and arms

UKRAINE

TAJIKISTAN

ARMENIA

KYRGYZSTAN

Braided hair of sheep's wool or beaten flax

Upper arms made of loosely stuffed cloth, sewn to body

Padded cloth cozy underneath skirt

DANCING COSSACK (LEFT)

This jolly character, c.1980, was inspired by one of Gogol's short stories. The head and lower arms are plastic, as are the lower legs, which are molded to show boots. The body, upper arms, and upper legs are stuffed cloth. Special features are the star-shaped hands and open mouth. Ht: 7½in (19cm)

Curly wool hat

Molded and painted mustache

Cotton blouse with printed "embroidery"

Woven fabric sash

Nylon trousers "tucked" into molded boots

Figure is fixed into dancing-on-heels position

YELTSIN

Solid wood is turned on a lathe, halved around the center, and hollowed out

GORBACHEV

BREZHNEV

KHRUSHCHEV

STALIN

LENIN

CZAR NICHOLAS II

1992 POLITICAL SEQUENCE (LEFT)

Nesting dolls have been made in Russia for centuries, yet the idea probably originated in China. The dolls usually represent famous characters, peasants, or animals. The smallest doll is solid wood. Ht: Largest 4¼in (11cm), smallest ½in (13mm)

РОССИЯ

СССР ПЕРЕСТРОЙ

Patriotic Character Dolls

· 1890s to 1918 ·

WHETHER MADE AS DIGNIFIED, true-to-life representations of their human counterparts, or as caricatures, patriotic dolls often mark a particular historical event or celebrate a country's pride in its national identity. Heads of state and war heroes are usually serious portrait dolls. The c.1840 Pierotti Queen Victoria (see page 37), for example, was the family's personal tribute to the monarch on her marriage to Prince Albert of Saxe-Coburg-Gotha. On the other hand, politicians – an age-old target for gibes and ridicule – are commonly shown as caricatures.

In the United States, one of the best-loved of all character dolls is the symbolic figure Uncle Sam. Traditionally depicted as an older man with an austere yet smiling face, white hair, a goatee, and always wearing the Stars and Stripes on some part of its clothing, this mascot is the male personification of the United States. The name is used, even today, to bring a touch of familiarity to official government language.

Stars on hatband match those on vest, and are adapted from the United States flag

Metal button, showing a 48-star flag, may be a later addition to the doll's costume

Clothing conceals composition or papier-mâché body, jointed at shoulders, elbows, hips, and knees

Felt material of top hat was originally blue, one of the colors of the United States flag

Molded and painted eyebrows

Hair and goatee are made of mohair, glued to the head and chin

Inset blue-gray glass eyes

Exaggerated features, typical of portraits of fictional characters

Back of the neck bears incised mark "S1," indicating the socket head is made by Simon and Halbig

Wrinkles and skin folds are defined with red paint

Lower torso is slightly padded in front, to make a small paunch

Metal "pocket watch" hangs from the vest on a striped ribbon fob

Head measures 3in (7.5cm) from crown to base of neck and 8in (20cm) around widest part of forehead

Single-breasted frock coat, made of blue felt, with metal buttons at front and back

GERMAN BISQUE UNCLE SAM *This version of the Uncle Sam character reflects one country's response to another's patriotic fervor. Using Simon and Halbig socket heads, the dolls were manufactured and marketed by Cuno and Otto Dressel of Sonneberg, Germany, in 1896. They were exported to the United States prior to the explosive start of the Spanish–American War in 1898.*

Patriotic red- and white-striped trousers

Black cloth "patent leather" shoes, decorated with metal buckles

Machine-knitted brown cotton socks

HT: 14in (35cm)

Composition socket head, with molded and painted hair

Painted intaglio eyes

Detailed replica of full-size uniform

1ST EARL KITCHENER OF KHARTOUM (ABOVE) Disabled British soldiers and seamen of World War I immortalized Lord Kitchener, Secretary of State, as a cloth-bodied doll with composition head, hands, and boots. Ht: 19in (48cm)

Uniform conceals stuffed cloth body

Composition socket head, with painted intaglio eyes

ALBERT I, KING OF THE BELGIANS (LEFT) Representing King Albert I of Belgium as Chief of Staff of the Belgian Army, this portrait doll was made in England in 1915. It is part of the same series as the doll portraying Lord Kitchener (see left). Ht: 19in (48cm)

Composition hands end just above wrist joint

WORLD WAR I TOMMY SOLDIER (RIGHT) Portrait dolls depict not only famous characters, but also those whose identities are unknown. Modeled as a boyish-looking young man, this c.1916 doll wears the khaki uniform of a private, or tommy, in the British Army. The cloth strips, or "puttees" as they are known, were a typical feature of soldiers' uniforms during World War I. Ht: 15in (38cm)

Chad Valley dolls often have a woven cloth label machine-stitched to the sole of the foot.

Head is made from stiffened, molded felt, with painted facial features and hair, and stitched ears

Felt clothing conceals unjointed cloth body, stuffed with kapok

STANLEY, 1ST EARL BALDWIN OF BEWDLEY (ABOVE) This rag doll, a caricature of a former British Conservative Prime Minister, is one of a series of political figures created by Chad Valley Co. Ltd. (see pages 98–99) in the 1930s. Ht: 12in (30cm)

1898 SPANISH–AMERICAN WAR HEROES (RIGHT) Doll-makers worldwide celebrated the United States victory in this 100-day war. According to museum records, these three portrait dolls were sent to the United States "compliments of Cuno and Otto Dressel, Sonneberg," at the request of the then U.S. Consul-General in Germany. Ht: 15in (38cm)

PRESIDENT WILLIAM McKINLEY

ADMIRAL GEORGE DEWEY

ADMIRAL WILLIAM THOMAS SAMPSON

Broadcloth uniforms, with epaulets, stripes, and insignia

Simon and Halbig bisque socket heads, with molded, painted hair and facial features

Uniforms conceal fully jointed composition bodies

Feet are molded and painted as boots

Unusual Dolls

In the world of dolls, there have always been a few that are strikingly out of the ordinary: they may have a unique feature of some kind, or have been made from an unusual material, or perhaps put to an intriguing use. One or two of the oddities described here are play dolls; but by far the most unusual are ornamental or display figures. Much sought after in their time, they are justifiably collectors' items today.

THE FINAL YEARS of the nineteenth century were a time of great creativity and energy in the world at large. In all sectors of industry and society, people were eager to experiment with an unusual idea, or to try the latest invention. In the design and manufacture of dolls, too, there were many innovations at this time: for example, lead-weighted sleeping eyes replaced the earlier push-pull wired type, and sound mechanisms allowed a doll to "speak." But probably one of the strangest was the introduction of multiple heads and faces. On some dolls, one head can be exchanged for another that has a different hairstyle or different expression, and perhaps even a different flesh tone.

The most popular dolls of this type, however, have a single head molded with two or three faces (see pages 142–143). The head is mounted on a spindle set into the torso, and the various faces are revealed by turning a handle on top of the head.

The Use of Metal

One development at this time was the use of metal. Mainly used for doll heads, metal was in some cases used for the whole figure. One of the major producers of metal heads was the German firm of Buschow and Beck. The heads were exported to England and the United States, where they were attached to stuffed cloth or composition bodies. The metal was usually coated tin, although painted brass and pewter were also used. The heads themselves were unbreakable, but the paintwork quickly discolored and was easily chipped. Such dolls soon fell out of favor.

Peddlers on Display

Some of the most unusual dolls are found among those intended primarily for display or as decoration. In England in the nineteenth century, there existed a fashion for dressing any doll that was on hand as a peddler. The character of the doll lay in its costume – a red hooded cloak, or a black or print dress, and white apron – and in the wicker tray or basket it carried, containing a wide variety of tiny household goods, knickknacks, and

BOUDOIR DOLL
(*LEFT*) *A boudoir doll reclines against damask cushions, resplendent in an exotic dress. This is an unusual model since it comes with several outfits. Most have only one, stitched to the body. Ht: 24in (60cm)*

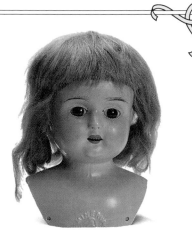

TEAPOT HALF DOLL (LEFT) This delicate half doll, holding flowers in her graceful arms, has been attached to a crocheted wool tea cozy. Made in Germany, the doll has molded hair and painted facial features. Doll ht: 2in (5cm)

METAL HEAD (RIGHT) This shoulder head bears the raised mark "MINERVA," a trade name of the German firm Buschow and Beck. Relatively few metal-headed dolls were made. Head ht: 4¾in (12cm)

notions (see pages 144–145). The majority of peddler dolls were dressed at home, but some were produced commercially, albeit on a small scale.

Half Dolls and Boudoir Dolls

Among the oddest phenomena are the half dolls produced during the 1920s and 1930s. These, too, were designed primarily as ornaments – but with a difference, since they were also used to disguise or decorate household objects. Consisting of a hollow head and torso, the half doll could be stitched or glued onto items such as tea cozies, hair and clothes brushes, dusting powder jars, even covers for the telephone. Virtually any material was used – wood, bisque, plastic – but most, by far, were made in porcelain, at factories in France, Germany, and Japan. Some half dolls are still made today, but the modern versions tend to be gaudy imitations of the originals.

～ It was at approximately the same time that the boudoir doll emerged, an essential accessory for the woman of fashion in Europe, as well as in the United States. Their long, lean bodies were made of composition or padded cloth over a wire frame, and their faces were molded and covered with painted silk or with stockinette. Resembling sultry-eyed "ladies," these beautiful dolls languished on beds, divans, sofas, and pianos. They soon became popular as mascots for taking along on car, train, or airplane journeys; young women would take them to dances, and even out visiting. Also called vamps, wobblies, or flappers in the United States, many boudoir dolls were dressed to represent the modern woman, in clothing that was the height of fashion in the 1920s: Charleston dresses, strings of beads, and cloche hats; mock fur coats; silken evening pajamas; long close-fitting satin gowns.

～ Weird and wonderful dolls are still being made today, in the tradition of the late nineteenth-century art dolls. E.J. Taylor, an American living in London, creates fascinating characters, modeling their strong, expressive features in a special craft clay (see pages 146–147). Designed solely for display, these dolls are regarded by many people as works of art.

LADY WITH HAT (LEFT) Of all half dolls, those portraying fashionable women of the 18th century were the most popular. This graceful figure is made of bisque, with painted features and gold decoration on the bodice of the dress. Ht: 8in (20cm)

POWDER PUFF LADY (BELOW) This bisque half doll, used as the cover for a box of dusting powder, has a crinoline-style costume made of strands of green wool, decorated with red. The elaborate wig is typical of such figures. Ht: 2¾in (7cm)

Multiple Heads and Faces

· 1860s to 1980s ·

FROM THE 1860s ONWARD, a number of patents were taken out for dolls with two or three different faces molded on the same head. Fritz Bartenstein and Carl Bergner, both of Germany, were among the major manufacturers of these in the nineteenth century, and Herr Bergner's firm continued until the 1930s. Although a doll with a range of facial expressions does allow play to be more realistic, the doll can look quite hideous because of the head cover that must extend from the shoulder plate to hide the "reserve" faces. The principle of changing faces is still used today, for example, in rag storybook dolls, which show the faces of different characters as the cloth pages are lifted.

Another similar, if less bizarre, novelty is the doll that has one body and a set of three or four different heads, which may represent a boy and a girl, each with a happy and a sad expression. Such a doll may also have interchangeable limbs, one set being made in a different flesh tone.

HT: 16in (40cm)

TWO-FACED DOLL *Probably made by Fritz Bartenstein in Germany in the 1880s, this doll has an egg-shaped head, molded with two faces and two sets of ears. The detail in the screaming face is pleasingly authentic: apart from the open mouth, the flesh tone is darker than that of the smiling doll, the eyebrows are knitted together into a frown, and the nostrils are red.*

Mohair wig is attached to the head cover

Composition swivel head coated in wax

Painted facial features; eyes are inset blown glass

Two-tiered cape, made of nun's veiling edged with crocheted cotton lace, with satin ribbon tie

Head is turned by a metal and wooden peg

Fabric-covered carton cap, molded as an extension of the composition shoulder plate

Cotton robe, with broderie anglaise bodice and flounces

Doll says "Mama" when voice box within torso is activated by pulling a cord at waist

Hands are painted composition; rest of limbs are made of wood and stuffed pink calico

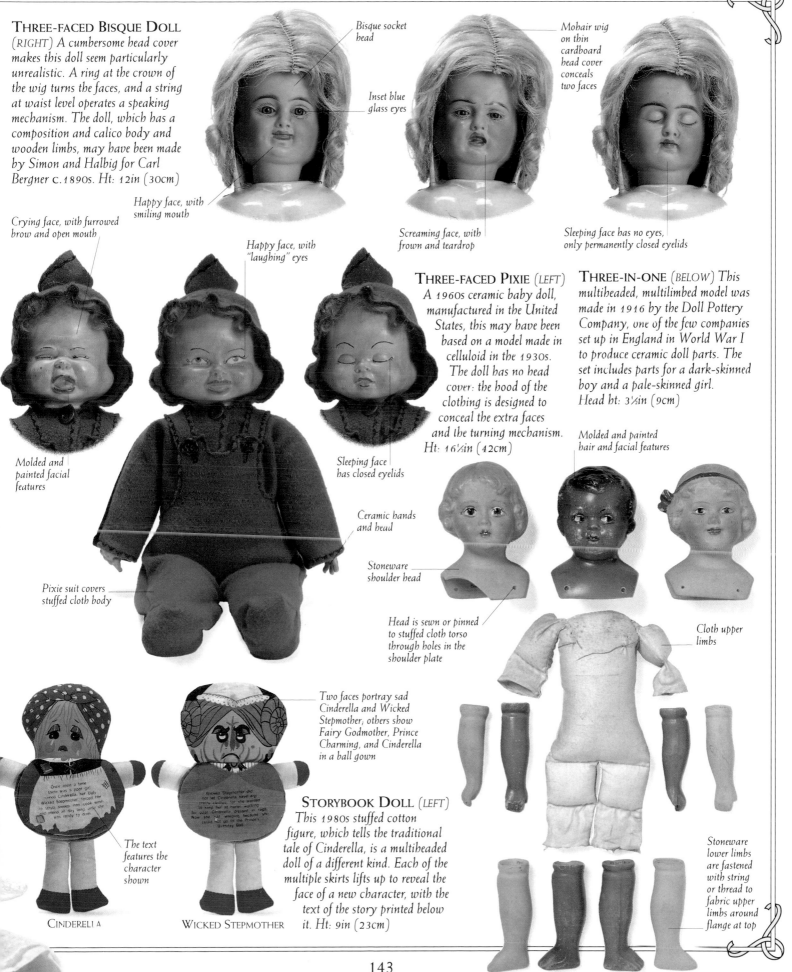

THREE-FACED BISQUE DOLL

(RIGHT) *A cumbersome head cover makes this doll seem particularly unrealistic. A ring at the crown of the wig turns the faces, and a string at waist level operates a speaking mechanism. The doll, which has a composition and calico body and wooden limbs, may have been made by Simon and Halbig for Carl Bergner c.1890s. Ht: 12in (30cm)*

Bisque socket head

Inset blue glass eyes

Happy face, with smiling mouth

Mohair wig on thin cardboard head cover conceals two faces

Screaming face, with frown and teardrop

Sleeping face has no eyes, only permanently closed eyelids

Crying face, with furrowed brow and open mouth

Happy face, with "laughing" eyes

Molded and painted facial features

THREE-FACED PIXIE (LEFT)

A 1960s ceramic baby doll, manufactured in the United States, this may have been based on a model made in celluloid in the 1930s. The doll has no head cover: the hood of the clothing is designed to conceal the extra faces and the turning mechanism. Ht: 16½in (42cm)

Sleeping face has closed eyelids

Ceramic hands and head

Pixie suit covers stuffed cloth body

THREE-IN-ONE (BELOW) *This*

multiheaded, multilimbed model was made in 1916 by the Doll Pottery Company, one of the few companies set up in England in World War I to produce ceramic doll parts. The set includes parts for a dark-skinned boy and a pale-skinned girl. Head ht: 3⅓in (9cm)

Molded and painted hair and facial features

Stoneware shoulder head

Head is sewn or pinned to stuffed cloth torso through holes in the shoulder plate

Cloth upper limbs

Two faces portray sad Cinderella and Wicked Stepmother; others show Fairy Godmother, Prince Charming, and Cinderella in a ball gown

The text features the character shown

STORYBOOK DOLL (LEFT)

This 1980s stuffed cotton figure, which tells the traditional tale of Cinderella, is a multiheaded doll of a different kind. Each of the multiple skirts lifts up to reveal the face of a new character, with the text of the story printed below it. Ht: 9in (23cm)

CINDERELLA

WICKED STEPMOTHER

Stoneware lower limbs are fastened with string or thread to fabric upper limbs around flange at top

Peddler Dolls

· 1820s to 1990s ·

AS A CONVERSATION PIECE in fashionable drawing rooms in nineteenth-century England, few objects could rival the fascinating peddler doll. Given a prominent place on a whatnot or the mantelpiece, and usually sitting beneath a glass dome to protect it from dust, the peddler doll would be dressed in the traditional red-cloaked costume, carrying a tray or basket overflowing with miniature wares. Most popular between 1820 and 1860, peddler dolls are enjoying a revival today.

Although itinerant traders traveled all over Europe, peddler dolls were a peculiarly English phenomenon. Even so, most were made in Germany and dressed in England. The heads are often wood or composition, but kid, apples, and wax were also used. The bodies are often made of wood, composition, or stuffed cloth.

The maker's mark is stamped in ink on the back of the torso.

Molded and painted facial features

Costume is typical of 19th-century female peddler

Bonnet is molded with the head and hair

Cap frill is made of lace dipped in slip, then fired with the head

Bisque shoulder head attached to the body by strips of sticky-backed fabric

Stuffed calico upper arms and torso; disk joints at shoulders

Bisque lower arms, cast to above wrists

Hands are large and gnarled, like those of an old woman

Stuffed calico upper legs, stitched to torso at hips

Bisque lower legs, with molded and painted stockings and shoes

Basket contents include bead necklaces, books, toys, and miniature dolls

MARTHA THOMPSON DOLL *Some peddler dolls came with an empty basket, to be filled at home with a variety of tiny items, ranging from notions to kitchenware. This peddler was made in the United States by Martha Thompson in the late 1960s, and dressed and equipped by English doll collector Faith Eaton in 1992.*

HT: 12in (30cm)

Gray mohair wig, glued on head

Spectacles made of copper wire

Simple painted facial features

Wooden head and torso, with peg-jointed limbs

Equipped with a wide range of knickknacks and miniature household utensils

APPLE-HEAD PEDDLER (RIGHT)
A pickled apple forms the head of this unusual peddler, which was made in England c.1830. The apple is carved and painted to re-create the wrinkled, weather-beaten features of an old street vendor. Ht: 6in (15cm)

Glass bead eyes set into pickled apple head

Open mouth showing teeth

PEG WOODEN PEDDLER (LEFT)
Made originally as a peg wooden, (see pages 18–19), this peddler dates from about 1900. It was adapted in the 1960s by Hilda Fonteyn, a doll enthusiast living in northern England. Ht: 13in (33cm)

Colorful clothing hides a crudely made cloth body

Inset silk hair

Painted facial features

Wax shoulder head, molded with bosom and arms

Doll is mounted on a varnished wooden stand

Painted hair and facial features

Carved wooden head and torso, with peg-jointed limbs

Original contents of basket can help to date the doll

"HENRIETTA" (RIGHT) Most peddler dolls represent old women, so this example of a young lady is particularly striking. The graceful wax-headed figure, with beautifully formed hands, was made c.1860 by English wax modeler Henrietta Wade. Ht: 10in (25cm)

NOTION NANNY
(RIGHT) Made in the United States c.1960s, this doll is said to represent a typical peddler of the Ozark mountain range, wandering through parts of Oklahoma, Arkansas, and Missouri. Notion Nanny is one of the names given to peddler dolls in the United States. Ht: 10½in (27cm)

Woven basket holds doll-size metal utensils

Padded cloth legs and torso over wire armature

Wooden mount is normally covered by glass dome, which sits in the groove

Soles of feet are painted to resemble shoes

A Master Doll-maker

· 1970s to the present day ·

TRAINED AS A COSTUME DESIGNER at Parsons School of Design in New York, E.J. Taylor began making dolls in 1973. The first models he created were clowns based on characters from Italy's commedia dell'arte theater. The following year he designed a group of half-man and half-animal figures. Then, in 1976, Taylor created a figure, which he called Lady in White, for Tiffany's jewelry store in New York, and this proved so successful that, two years later, Saks Fifth Avenue asked the artist to produce three more "garden ladies."

Taylor's dolls all have an extraordinary quality: their heads and hands are modeled from Sculpey, a craft clay material developed in the United States that can be fired to a ceramic-like hardness at household oven temperatures; the bodies are made of papier-mâché molded over a wire armature.

Half-closed eyes with heavy eyelids, accentuated with peach coloring

Well-shaped hands with long, elegant fingers, modeled in Sculpey

Straw bonnet is tinted to match the delicate tones of the painted facial features

Traditional Sussex trug contains dried roses

Facial features, modeled from Sculpey clay, have a lifelike quality

Closed, full-lipped mouth is drawn back and indented at the corners

High, spare cheekbones; slackened jaw shows "bone" structure beneath

Clothes conceal body made of papier-mâché molded over a wire armature

Damask silk costume made from a fringed shawl, trimmed with bead buttons

LADY IN WHITE *The first of a group of four "garden ladies," the Lady in White was designed and made by E.J. Taylor in 1976, as a display piece for Tiffany's jewelry store in New York City. The figure portrays an elderly, aristocratic-looking woman dressed in a costume reminiscent of those worn in the early decades of the 20th century.*

HT: 30in (77cm)

Facial features are
modeled and painted;
human hair wig

Sculpey
shoulder
head

Branching twigs
form the antlers
of the reindeer

Elf's outfit is made from
scraps of fur, fabric,
and leather

Papier-mâché
body – Sculpey
is too heavy to be
used for whole doll

Sculpey hands
encased in
crocheted
mittens

Painted hair and
facial features

Finely modeled head
captures the strong
features of a young
girl of African origin

Wire armature
provides the
skeleton
of the doll

Papier-mâché legs,
wearing stockings

DOLL IN THE MAKING

(RIGHT) The construction of this
figure is typical of Taylor's work.
The head, hands, and feet are
modeled from Sculpey clay, while
the rest of the body and legs are
made of papier-mâché over a wire
armature. Ht: 27½in (70cm)

Huge flat
feet and
sticklike legs

Sculpey feet, with
shaped instep and
heel, allow the doll
to stand unaided

JESSIE (ABOVE) This fine head
was created in 1988, using Sculpey
III – a clay that has all the features
of Super Sculpey, with the bonus of
being available in 30 colors. The
finished texture of the clay gives the
illusion that the figure is made of
wax. Head ht: 4in (10cm)

ELF (ABOVE) Created as part
of a Christmas window display
commissioned by Tiffany's, New
York, in 1981, the elf is riding a
stuffed stockinette "hobby horse"
reindeer with twig antlers, which
is also the work of Taylor. The
elf's head is made of Super
Sculpey, a type of flesh-
tone craft clay with a
ceramic-like finish.
Ht: 11in (28cm)

MAN
Ht: 13in
(33cm)

Clothing made
from scraps of net,
lace, silk, burlap,
and other fabrics

GROUP OF THREE (LEFT)
Produced in 1981 for Tiffany's
Christmas window display, this trio
represents three ages of mankind.
Taylor also designed and made the
clothing for the dolls. The male
figure, including the hair, is
finished in varying shades
of one color, while the two
women are dressed in
neutral tones, with added
vibrance in the old lady's
bonnet and the young
woman's stomacher.

OLD
WOMAN
Ht: 13in
(33cm)

Expressive
hands are a
feature of E.J.
Taylor dolls

Cotton jacket
knitted by
E.J. Taylor

YOUNG
WOMAN
Ht: 12in
(30cm)

Crocheted
cotton
slippers

Useful Information

Most collections have modest beginnings: a doll from childhood, or perhaps one found in the attic, which belonged to your mother or grandmother, or one bought at random, simply because you liked the look of it. A mild curiosity about the history of one particular doll sparks an interest in the whole fascinating subject — an interest that may soon become an all-consuming passion, even taking over your home and your life.

THE MAJORITY OF BEGINNERS tend to acquire each and every doll they see; gradually they become more selective, developing a liking for certain kinds of doll and choosing these in preference to all others. As you become more knowledgeable, through books, lectures, clubs, and exhibitions, you may decide to specialize, perhaps choosing dolls of a particular material or ones created by an individual or a single company; or you may collect only portrait dolls or dolls with fancy molded hair. Even collectors of modern dolls often limit the selection to just one type.

〜 As soon as you have started your own collection, however modest, you should consider not only how to house it, but also how to look after it (see pages 150–153). It is sensible to think carefully before amassing a very large collection. You may soon find that your entire home has become a display cabinet.

Where and What to Buy

If you are a beginner, it is advisable to buy your dolls from a reputable auction house, such as Christie's or Sotheby's, or a well-established doll dealer. The big auction houses have salesrooms or affiliated branches in many parts of the world. If you are in any doubt about a dealer's reputation, be sure to consult another, more experienced collector, or check with your local doll club. Collecting modern dolls is much easier, of course, as you simply buy the doll directly from the maker, or if it is a mass-produced doll, from your local

COLLECTIBLE WAX (*LEFT*) *A lovely wax doll such as this figure, made in the 1890s by Lucy Peck (see page 35), can be bought at a relatively low price because of the general belief that wax is unstable. Although wax is affected by changes in its surroundings, a sudden drop in temperature is the most damaging. Ht: 20in (50cm)*

ORIGINAL BOXED SET (*RIGHT*) *Acquiring a doll in its original state is a joy for any collector. The doll in this bisque set, made in the late 19th century by J.D. Kestner of Germany, is still tied to its box around the ankles, and at the waist underneath the apron. Ht: 18in (46cm)*

JUMEAU MÉDAILLE D'OR PARIS

Ink stamp, usually found on the back of the torso

GERMAIN No 4 30

Molded mark on celluloid head

Incised mark on bisque head

FABRICATION FRANCAISE S.F.B.J. PARIS

Paper label

"ANGELITA" U. F. OF DOLL CLUBS LOS ANGELES · 1963

Cloth label, stitched to clothes

EINE SCHILDKRÖT-PUPPE MODELL Käthe Kruse

Wrist tag, found only on 20th-century dolls

IDENTIFYING MARKS (ABOVE)

From the 1890s, international law decreed that dolls (in common with all other products) must be marked or labeled with their country of origin. Marks and labels also help to date a doll and identify its maker, as well as the model. Head marks sometimes include a mold number. Corresponding size numbers may also appear on the head and body.

MISGUIDED IMPROVEMENT

(RIGHT) This fine bisque swivel head doll, made c. 1890 by the Parisian company Bru Jne. and Cie, has been spoiled by replacing the original mohair wig with a modern nylon one, which is both too large and too heavy. Dolls that have suffered "improvements" like this may cost less to buy than others.

the French bisque dolls of the 1860s to 1880s; all dolls made by the French houses of Bru and Jumeau; and so-called character dolls.

Even if you have a limited budget, you need not hesitate to start collecting dolls. A good collection can be created using dolls made from the 1930s onward. Some nineteenth-century dolls are also quite modestly priced, notably those of wax and wax-over-composition, and the peg wooden dolls.

Gathering Information

When you acquire a doll, try to seek out as much information about it as you can: any known family history; who owned the doll before you and when; and if it has a name, either the maker's trade name or one given by a former owner. Anything that happens to a doll while it is in your care, for example getting new clothing or receiving repairs, should also be noted.

~ Collecting dolls does require an investment, of both time and money. However, you will find that dolls can open up several new avenues of interest – in fashion, architecture, interior design. Even after years of collecting and enjoying dolls, they will still be able to stir your imagination and bring you great pleasure.

store. As your knowledge increases, so will your ability to judge the quality, condition, and value of any doll you see. After a while, if you decide that you wish to refine your collection, it makes good sense to build up a network with other collectors, since many are willing to swap dolls instead of buying or selling them.

~ It is impossible to give a definitive guide to dolls worth collecting: the market is changeable, and styles of dolls go in and out of fashion almost at random. In general, however, the most sought after, and therefore the most expensive, dolls are the wooden ones made in the late seventeenth and early eighteenth centuries;

A SPECIALIST'S DELIGHT

(RIGHT) Many people choose to specialize in their own collections, concentrating on dolls of one type or material, or those of one maker or one country. This Japanese boxed set, made in 1912, would be a real find for anyone focusing on oriental dolls: clothing and accessories accompany the figures (see page 133), and the whole set is in excellent condition, with every piece intact. A set like this is likely to command a high price, not only because of its quality, but also because it may be of interest to those collecting other oriental artifacts.

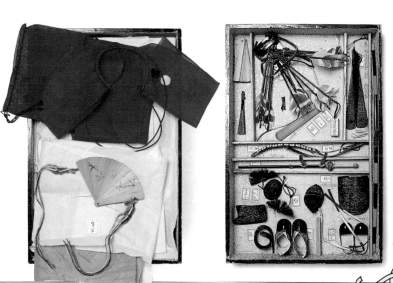

Caring For Your Collection
· Conservation and Restoration ·

IT IS CRUCIAL TO KEEP your doll collection in the right conditions. Most importantly, protect the dolls from sunlight, dust, and smoke from cigarettes or open fires. Dramatic changes in temperature cause major damage, so try to maintain the room at an even, but warmish, temperature, preferably somewhere between 65°F and 70°F (18–21°C), and keep the dolls away from hot-water pipes and radiators, or any source of heat.

You will not, of course, want to leave your dolls permanently on the shelf, but bear in mind that the less they are handled the better – not only to reduce the risk of damage, but also to prevent soiling from the natural oils in your skin. If you choose to wear cotton gloves when handling your dolls, wash them often to ensure that they are scrupulously clean.

Check your dolls regularly for signs of wear and tear; this will give you a better chance of arresting any problem – such as an attack of woodworm – before it becomes serious. If your dolls do need some form of repair, be guided by the expert advice of a professional doll restorer: inappropriate replacement parts or badly done work may ruin a doll, and even reduce its value.

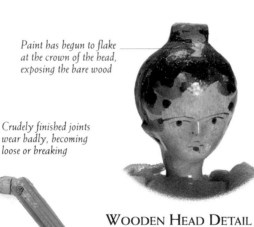

Paint has begun to flake at the crown of the head, exposing the bare wood

Crudely finished joints wear badly, becoming loose or breaking

Hole in chest made by woodworm

Paint applied directly to the wood has no sound base and quickly begins to deteriorate

Damaged leg caused by rough and careless handling

WOODEN HEAD DETAIL
(ABOVE) Flaking paint can be a major problem with old wooden dolls. In the 18th century, the wood was given a gesso base before it was painted; but later, in order to cut costs, the paint was applied directly to the wood. A slight bump can start the flaking process, which, if unchecked, will continue until all the paint has disappeared.

WOOD (LEFT)
THE QUALITY of wooden dolls deteriorated in the 19th and 20th centuries. Such dolls were rather crudely crafted and painted, and were not expected to become "antiques." Among the parts commonly damaged are the pegs in the joints: these are very small wooden pins, which snap extremely easily. The tenons of the joints may wear, too, or may even break off altogether.

RAG WITH COMPOSITION (BELOW)
ALL RAG DOLLS HAVE SIMILAR problems, many of which are caused by the way their owners handle them, rather than by any flaw in the construction of the doll. Soft rag dolls tend to be hugged and played with a good deal, especially by younger children. The areas most likely to be damaged are the parts that stick out – the nose and toes – and those that are pulled – the arms and the legs. With the example below, perhaps the doll's saving grace is that it has not suffered from "restoration," which can inflict as much damage as it attempts to repair.

Painted surface of the composition head is badly crazed and chipped

Tip of the nose is chipped, exposing the composition beneath

Fabric of the body is soiled, especially on the arms and legs

Left arm is split just above the wrist, and stuffing is leaking

Soles of the feet are worn, revealing inner cardboard stiffening

Composition shoulder head has severe crack across the top

Projecting parts, such as the tip of the nose, are easily chipped

Upper cloth arm has lost its stuffing

Dark stains on rag torso indicate that the doll has been very wet at some time, probably causing the stuffing to deteriorate

Composition fingers on left arm are chewed

Seams at feet have split, allowing the stuffing to leak out

Lower composition arm is completely missing

Extremities are liable to suffer the most wear and tear

COMPOSITION WITH RAG (LEFT)

THIS CANADIAN DOLL from the late 1930s or early 1940s has been damaged from head to toe, probably through its owner's enthusiasm rather than from neglect. The doll appears to have been given a thorough soaking at some point – it may even have been bathed. This would have caused the composition, and the body stuffing, to disintegrate.

Parts of the thick outer coating of wax have broken away, leaving features such as the nose vulnerable to damage

Composition base has shrunk away from its wax coating

WAX-OVER-COMPOSITION (ABOVE)

THE TECHNIQUE of using wax over molded composition developed as a means of making heads with the look of expensive poured wax, at a fraction of the cost. A major problem of this combination, however, is the different rates at which the two materials expand and contract. As this occurs, the wax cracks and, in severe cases, large sections may fall away.

Inset hair has been damaged; overly vigorous brushing, insect infestation, or shaving are the most obvious causes

PLASTIC (RIGHT)

MODERN PLASTICS are durable materials, but earlier types, such as celluloid, slowly disintegrate as they age. If a plastic doll is to last, it must be looked after as carefully as if it were made of bisque or wax. Hard plastics are brittle and liable to break; if painted, the surface may chip away, and worn or pitted plastic is not easily cleaned.

Nylon wig is tangled and matted

Dirt has become ingrained in the plastic, especially on the face and in the crevices in the hands and feet

Neck is split on one side, along the mold line

Shoulder plate is broken and some parts of it are missing

Broken edges of the wax are distorted

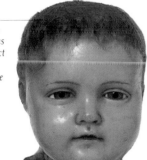

POURED WAX (ABOVE)

THE MOST EASILY DAMAGED PART of a poured wax head is the neck, where the wax is thinnest, so never grasp a doll only by its neck. Dropping or knocking it on a hard surface will cause the wax to break. If the break is a clean one, an expert restorer may be able to repair it. However, as in this late 19th-century shoulder head, sometimes the wax twists and becomes slightly misshapen so that the edges will not fit together exactly.

CELLULOID ARM

DETAIL (ABOVE) Repairing plastics that have split along a seam is possible; but if the crack occurs elsewhere, for example on the lower arm, as in the detail shown above, there is little that you can do. It is not a good idea to use glue, as this may cause a chemical reaction between the glue and elements in the plastic.

Belly has caved in, probably under the weight of a child, or a chair

BISQUE WITH COMPOSITION (RIGHT)

THE WAY IN WHICH A DOLL IS STRUNG can be the cause of major problems. Ideally, the stringing should be tight enough to keep the head from falling, but loose enough to allow the joints to move freely. In the case of this doll, made in France *c.*1900, too-tight stringing has caused friction at the joints of the torso and limbs, whose surfaces are badly worn. In general, the painted finish on later composition doll bodies, such as this one, is poorer than on earlier models. The doll's bisque socket head also needs some skilled care and attention: a crack runs from the hairline through the right eyebrow and down the side of the nose; and the sleeping glass eyes have fallen or been pushed into the head itself.

Bisque is cracked from hairline to side of nose

Teeth are missing from the mouth

Head has been broken from body, but has remained in one piece

Loose stringing causes joints to collapse

Hardened glue from an earlier repair; trying to remove it could damage the head further

Left and right arms have broken off and are missing

Composition is exposed and will gradually deteriorate

SLEEPING EYES MECHANISM

(RIGHT) Dabs of plaster hold the mechanism to the head. If the doll is stored on its back, the weight of the mechanism weakens the plaster fixing, and the eyes fall backward.

Blown glass paperweight eyes set in bisque surround

Human hair lashes glued to the tops of the eyes

Lead weight hangs between the eyes and controls their movement

Mohair wig is matted and sparse in places

Eyes have fallen inside head, dolls with lead-weighted sleeping eyes should be stored facedown, on suitable padding to prevent abrasion

COMPOSITION FINGERS

(BELOW) Composition fingers are vulnerable to damage, especially if molded separately, since they snap off easily. Repairs are hard to make, because the fingers are so small and have no internal support on which replacement parts could be built.

Paint on fingers is cracked and flaking

Too-tight stringing has resulted in an elongated hole, as torso and leg have rubbed together

Friction at the joint has caused varnish and paint to wear away, exposing the bare composition

Ball joint has come loose

Paintwork is subject to damage around ball joints at knees, wrists, and elbows, as well as at strung body parts

ALL-BISQUE (ABOVE) By far

the greatest harm that can befall a bisque doll is being dropped or knocked against any hard surface: the bisque may fracture or shatter, or parts may be broken off altogether, as with this untinted bisque boy, made in Germany toward the end of the 19th century. Repairs are possible, but only with the use of special glues. Take great care when handling the pieces, as the broken edges may be jagged.

COMPOSITION LOWER LEGS

(BELOW) Composition toes tend to suffer the same kind of damage as fingers, although the toes are easier to repair because they are usually molded together. Shoes normally offer some protection; but the doll shown here has only molded and painted footwear, and the end of one foot has broken away completely.

Paint on feet is damaged, and toes are worn away

STUFFED KID *(BELOW and RIGHT)*

KID DOLLS SUFFER MOST when kept in hot, dry conditions, as the skin loses its natural oils, becoming brittle and crazed. Eventually the kid will split, usually at a seam since it is here that the strain is greatest. This in turn allows the stuffing to seep out, which can eventually spoil the shape of the whole doll. Very damp conditions also affect kid, causing mold growth or mildew; and both the kid and its stuffing are also vulnerable to attack by pests such as insects and mice.

KID LEGS *(LEFT)* Ankle joints on kid dolls are usually formed by inserting an additional piece of kid between the leg and the foot. In this case, the ankle piece has come unstitched and the foot is breaking off, allowing the sawdust stuffing to leak out. Any repair like this is best left to a professional, to ensure that the kid is securely replaced and the shape of the doll is fully restored.

KID HANDS *(RIGHT)* A stuffed kid doll often has a wire armature providing the basic form. Over time, as the joints are bent, the metal breaks and may burst through the stuffing and puncture the skin. This tends to happen most at the smallest, narrowest parts of the body, such as the wrists. The wire may also rust and twist, damaging the kid skin.

KID JOINTS *(LEFT)* In a pinned joint, such as this shoulder, the pins often work loose. As this happens, the kid around the pin tends to split. In this case, the damage has been compounded by covering the hole with an adhesive bandage, which it is impossible to remove without causing further harm.

Wire armature has broken through the kid covering

Kid has become crazed and brittle from being kept in hot, dry conditions

CLOTHING *(BELOW and RIGHT)*

THE CLOTHING OF DOLLS that are used as toys will, inevitably, be subject to general wear and tear. But even the clothes of display dolls can deteriorate if they are not kept in the right conditions. All fabrics have a natural rate of degeneration, but this can be exacerbated by excessive heat and damp; by the effect of the ultraviolet rays of the sun; and by attacks by mice or insects such as moths, beetles, and woodworm (which eat sawdust and straw stuffing as well as wood). Establishing a routine for checking your dolls will give you the best chance of remedying a problem before it gets out of hand.

MOLD *(LEFT)* Mold thrives in damp conditions, and the spotting that results can ruin clothing made of natural fibers such as silk. In the case of wax dolls, similar damage is sometimes caused when chemicals in the dye that was used to color the wax adversely affect the fabric.

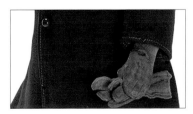

SILK *(LEFT)* Chemicals used in manufacturing silk may hasten the natural deterioration of the fabric. The most common result of this is "laddering," the threaded effect as the fibers disintegrate; at worst, the silk will literally turn to dust.

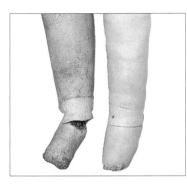

MOTHS *(LEFT)* Dolls and their clothing seem particularly attractive to insects and rodents, which can do irreparable harm. Examine your dolls regularly for signs of attack, but seek advice from a doll expert before carrying out any treatment.

LEATHER *(LEFT)* Like any other natural material, leather begins to deteriorate after some time, getting dry and brittle so that the surface cracks and breaks up. Oiling the leather will help keep it supple and also improve its appearance.

SUNLIGHT *(LEFT)* The sun's ultraviolet rays can damage dolls made of most materials, including plastic. Fading of the clothing is the most obvious result. Be sure that your dolls always sit safely out of direct sunlight, or use ultraviolet screens on your windows.

Color of dress has faded through exposure to sunlight

Original, brighter, richer color of dress

Addresses

MUSEUMS

BETHNAL GREEN MUSEUM OF CHILDHOOD
(A branch of the Victoria & Albert Museum)
Cambridge Heath Road
London, England E2 9PA, UK
Telephone 011 44 81 980 3204

~

MARGARET WOODBURY STRONG MUSEUM
1 Manhattan Square
Rochester, N.Y. 14607, USA
Telephone (716) 263-2700

~

MUSEUM OF CHILDHOOD
42 High Street
Edinburgh, Scotland EH1 1TG, UK
Telephone 011 44 31 225 2424

~

MUSEUM OF DOLL ART
1116 108th Avenue North East
Bellevue, WA 98006, USA
Telephone (206) 455-1116

~

POLLOCK'S TOY MUSEUM
1 Scala Street
London, England W1P 1LT, UK
Telephone 011 44 71 636 3452

~

WARWICK DOLL MUSEUM
Okens House
Castle Street
Warwick, Warwickshire CV34 4BP, UK
Telephone 011 44 926 495546/412500

WENHAM HISTORICAL ASSOCIATION AND MUSEUM
132 Main Street
Wenham, MA 01984, USA
Telephone (508) 468 2377

~

WORTHING MUSEUM & ART GALLERY
Chapel Road
Worthing, West Sussex BN11 1HP, UK
Telephone 011 44 903 239999

CLUBS

THE DOLL CLUB OF GREAT BRITAIN
Mrs. Jane Dunne, Unity Cottage,
Pishill Bank, Henley-on-Thames,
Oxfordshire RG9 6HJ, UK

~

DOLL COLLECTORS OF AMERICA
c/o Diane Buck
Wenham Historical Association
and Museum
see address above

~

DOLLOLOGY
affiliated to United Federation of Doll Clubs
see address below

~

UNITED FEDERATION OF DOLL CLUBS
10920 North Ambassador Drive
Kansas City, MO 64153, USA
Telephone (816) 891-7040

MAGAZINES

AUSTRALIAN DOLL DIGEST
Box 680
Goulburn, NSW 2580, Australia
Telephone 011 61 48 213660

~

BRITISH DOLL COLLECTORS NEWS
The Anchorage
Wrotham Road, Colverston
Meopham, Kent DA13 0QW, UK

~

DOLL CRAFTER
30595 Eight Mile
Livonia, MI 48152, USA

~

DOLL READER
Cumberland Publishing, Inc.
900 Frederick Street
Cumberland, MD 21502, USA
Telephone (301) 759-3770

~

DOLLS – THE COLLECTOR'S MAGAZINE
Collector Communications, Inc.
170 Fifth Avenue
New York, N.Y. 10010, USA
Telephone (212) 989 8700

~

U.K. DOLL DIRECTORY
Hugglets
P.O. Box 290
Brighton, East Sussex BN2 1DR, UK
Telephone 011 44 273 697974

Further Reading

Anderton, Johana Gast *Twentieth Century Dolls, From Bisque to Vinyl*, Trojan Press Inc., North Kansas City, MO 1971
Cieslik, Jürgen and Marianne *Dolls, European Dolls 1800–1930*, Christie's South Kensington Collectors' Guides, Studio Vista, London 1979

1850S ENGLISH WAX GIRL *This doll has a shoulder head of poured wax, with inset human hair and glass eyes. Its leather lower arms and calico body are all stuffed with cowhair. Ht: 18in (46cm)*

Cieslik, Jürgen and Marianne *German Doll Encyclopedia 1800–1939*, Hobby House Press, Cumberland, MD 1985
Coleman, Dorothy S., Elizabeth A., and Evelyn J. *The Collector's Encyclopedia of Dolls, Vols I and II*, Crown Publishers, Inc., New York 1968 and 1986
Eaton, Faith *Care & Repair of Antique & Modern Dolls*, B.T. Batsford Limited, London 1985
Eaton, Faith *Dolls in Colour*, Blandford Press, Poole 1975
Goodfellow, Caroline G. *Understanding Dolls*, Antique Collectors' Club, Woodbridge 1983
Mansell, Colette *The Collector's Guide to British Dolls Since 1920*, Robert Hale Ltd., London 1983

Glossary

AMERICAN CLOTH/OILCLOTH
Heavy woven cotton or linen
painted with oil-based paints.

BALL AND SOCKET JOINT Made
by fitting a rounded ball into a
concave socket. Usually seen on
composition and plastic bodies.

BENT LIMBS Curved arms and
legs, molded as complete units,
seen on baby doll bodies.

BISQUE Unglazed **porcelain**.

CELLULOID A synthetic material
based on vegetable fibers mixed
with nitric and sulfuric acids and
additives; flammable.

CLOSED MOUTH Lips are joined
and molded together, with no
open space between.

CLOTH Common term for any
linen or cotton fabric.

COMPOSITION Wood and/or
paper pulp mixed with additives.
Includes papier-mâché.

ERZGEBIRGE Region of eastern
Germany south of Dresden on
the Czech border, producing
carved wooden toys and dolls
in the 19th and 20th centuries.

FELT Matted wool fiber fabric.

FLANGE NECK HEAD Neck edge
of head curves outward. Usually
seen on stuffed cloth bodies.

FLIRTY EYES Combination of
sleeping eyes and eyes that move
to the side or from side to side.

GESSO Fine mix of plaster and
water or **size** applied over wood
as a base for paint finishes.

GLAZED CHINA Porcelain with
a shiny, high-gloss overglaze.

GOFUN Japanese material made
from crushed oyster shells and
additives; has a pearl-like finish.

GOOGLY EYES Eyes that glance
to only one side; sometimes
combined with **sleeping eyes**.
Also known as roguish eyes.

GRÖDENER TAL Region on the
borders of Austria, Germany, and
Italy; now part of Italy. Produced
carved wooden dolls in the 19th
and early 20th centuries.

MOTORING MISS *A German
bisque doll models this* c.1900
*costume for London's Marshall and
Snelgrove store. Ht: 12in (30cm)*

GROMMET Metal eyelet. Usually
seen only on poured wax dolls.

GUSSETED JOINT Made by inserting a V-shaped panel at elbow,
thigh, and knee joints. Usually
seen on kid and **rag** dolls.

INSET EYES Glass eyes set into
the eye sockets; cannot move.

INTAGLIO EYES Molded or
carved concave eyes, with
painted pupils and irises.

KAPOK Plant material similar to
cotton, used for stuffing.

LOWER ARM From elbow to
wrist; usually includes hand.

LOWER LEG From knee to ankle;
usually includes foot.

MORTISE AND TENON JOINT
Made by fitting tongues from
one part into grooves in another.
Usually seen on wooden bodies.

OPEN MOUTH Lips are cut open
after molding. May include teeth
and/or a molded tongue.

OPEN/CLOSED MOUTH Lips are
molded open but not cut. May
include a molded tongue.

PARIAN *See* **untinted bisque**.

PEGGED JOINT Simple **mortise
and tenon joint**, held by a peg.
Usually seen on early wooden
dolls and later cheap models.

PLASTIC Any synthetic material
that is malleable when soft and
can be molded into set forms.

PORCELAIN Fine-grade ceramic
material, fired at not less than
2,372°F (1,300°C).

RAG Any fabric material.

REVERSE SOCKET HEAD Head
ends below chin. Jointed to a
torso that extends upward from
the shoulders to form the neck.
Usually made of composition.
See also **socket head**.

SHOULDER HEAD Head, neck,
shoulders, and front and back
chest plates are built as one unit;
head cannot turn. May be made
of any material, in particular
poured wax or **porcelain**, but
generally not **rag**. *See also*
shoulder plates.

SHOULDER PLATES Front and
back chest parts of a **shoulder
head**. *See also* **swivel head**.

SIZE Thin, gelatinous mix, often
including glue, used as a surface
sealer. Component of **gesso**.

SLEEPING EYES Glass eyes that
open and shut mechanically so
that the doll appears to sleep.

SOCKET HEAD Head is molded
to include the neck, shaped at
the end as a ball. Jointed to a
torso with a cup-shaped socket
between the shoulders, into
which the head fits. Usually
made of **bisque** or **composition**.
See also **reverse socket head**.

SONNEBERG Principal town of
Thuringia in Germany. Trading
center of the doll industry until
the end of the 1930s.

STOCKINETTE Machine-knitted,
stretchy silk or cotton fabric.

SWIVEL HEAD Combination of a
shoulder and **socket** head. Neck
is included as part of the head,
which fits into separately cast
shoulder plates; head can turn.
Usually made of **glazed china**
or **bisque**.

THURINGIA *Thüringen* Region
of Germany to the north of
Bavaria. Location of most
of the **porcelain** factories
that produced doll heads
and limbs in the 19th
and 20th centuries.

TUCKCOMB/COMB High, carved
ornament on the crown of early
19th-century wooden doll heads,
resembling a small mantilla.

UNTINTED BISQUE Matte-finish
porcelain, usually white. Also
known as parian, particularly
in the United States.

UPPER ARM From the elbow to
the shoulder or shoulder joint.

UPPER LEG From the knee to the
hip or hip joint.

VELVET Woven silk fabric, with
a close, soft texture, short, dense
pile, and lustrous sheen.

VELVETEEN Similar to **velvet**, but
made of cotton rather than silk,
and lacking the lustrous sheen.

VINYL Post-1945 **plastic**; when
set, may be hard or soft.

WAX-OVER-COMPOSITION
Molded **composition**, coated
with a thin layer of wax to create
the appearance of poured wax.
Used for limbs as well as heads.

WORSTED Woven fabric made
of long-staple wool, with a close,
hard texture and no pile.

Index

DAVY CROCKETT *Designed and produced in 1955 by Vogue Dolls, Inc., this hard plastic doll portrays one of the most famous American folk heroes. Its imitation buckskin suit and rabbit fur hat provide an authentic outfit. Ht: 8in (20cm)*

CHINESE BOY *This pressed felt doll with painted facial features, thought to be the work of Lenci or Chad Valley, was made in Europe in the 1930s. The fine black mohair stitched to its head extends to form a long braid. Ht: 26in (65cm)*

DOLLY FACE GIRL *The bisque socket head and jointed composition body of this doll are typical of those made by the Société Française de Fabrication de Bébés et Jouets in the early years of the 20th century. Ht: 15in (38cm)*

GEBRÜDER HEUBACH GIRL
*Best known for its character babies,
the German company of Gebrüder
Heubach also created many other
lines, including this c.1920s girl
with dolly face. Ht: 16in (40cm)*

QUEEN ELIZABETH II *This bisque shoulder head was modeled in 1970 by Martha Thompson, a doll artist in the United States. The doll's lower arms and legs are also made of bisque, attached to a stuffed calico body. Doll ht: 14in (35cm)*

ORIENTAL GIRL *The bisque socket head of this late 19th-century German doll bears the mark of Schoenau and Hoffmeister. Ht: 14in (35cm)*

～ Acknowledgments ～

AUTHOR'S ACKNOWLEDGMENTS

My very grateful thanks to the Wenham Historical Association and Museum, Worthing Museum & Art Gallery, Christie's South Kensington, and Bethnal Green Museum of Childhood for their valuable assistance and cooperation; also Diane Buck, Sally White, Olivia Bristol, Christine Jeffery, Noreen Marshall, Betty Ridley, William Birnbaum, and Josephine Goodfellow. I especially thank Faith Eaton, for allowing the use of her wonderful dolls and for commenting on the text. Likewise, Dorothy and Evelyn Jane Coleman, my American family, deserve special thanks for sharing their vital knowledge as well as their beautiful dolls.
I am indebted to everyone at Dorling Kindersley for all their help, in particular Gillian Roberts, my good-humored editor, and Kevin Ryan, who has designed a magnificent book. Many thanks also to Matthew Ward in England and Lynton Gardiner in the United States for their inspired photographs. Finally, to Tiber and Miss Polly, thank you for being so patient.

PUBLISHER'S ACKNOWLEDGMENTS

Dorling Kindersley acknowledges the generous help of those individuals without whom this book could not have been produced. Special thanks to Catherine Sidwell at Bethnal Green Museum of Childhood; Katherine Higgins at Christie's South Kensington; and Linda Stiles and Sally White at Worthing Museum & Art Gallery. Polly Boyd and Lesley Riley worked diligently and with great patience to complete the text pages, supported by Constance Novis; Alex Corrin compiled the index; Charlotte Davies, Alison Edmonds, Chris Legee, and Alison Shackleton provided the team with creature comforts; Sharon Moore helped prepare pages for final film; Julia Pashley researched the archive picture material; Mel Roberts explained the ins and outs of the English language; Ann Thompson gave design assistance; Alastair Wardle contributed his computer expertise.

PUBLIC AND PRIVATE DOLL COLLECTIONS

In the following acknowledgments, abbreviations with page numbers indicate position on page:

t=top; b=bottom; c=center; l=left; r=right

All the dolls photographed for this book belong to the private collection of **Faith Eaton**, except: **Bethnal Green Museum of Childhood** *A branch of the Victoria & Albert Museum* 2, 7 (r), 12 (l, r), 13 (tl, bl, br), 16, 17 (3 dolls bl), 30 (l), 33 (tl, cr), 36, 37, 38, 39 (except bl, br), 40, 41, 57 (2 dolls tr), 60, 65 (bl), 70 (l, r), 71 (br), 79 (br), 84, 85 (tr), 96, 107 (bl), 115 (br), 119 (except tc), 124, 125, 129 (b), 131 (b), 136, 139 (2 dolls tl), 143 (br). **Christie's South Kensington** 61 (tl, tr, bl), 101 (br), 148 (br), 149 (tr), 150 (br). **Coleman Collection** 3, 42 (br), 43 (bl), 44, 45 (except tl), 46, 47 (except br), 48, 49 (tl, bl, bc, br), 50, 51 (tr, tc, c, br), 93 (tr), 97, 99 (tr), 101 (tl, tr). **Wenham Historical Association and Museum** 1, 6 (br), 9 (tl), 14, 15 (tl, bl), 17 (br), 22, 23 (c, br), 26, 27 (tl, tc, b), 32, 74 (r), 75, 88, 90, 91 (tl, bl, br), 92 (bc), 93 (5 dolls b), 104 (br), 105 (br), 106, 107 (tr, r), 111 (tl, tc), 112, 113 (tl, tc, bl, br), 122 (cl), 127 (tl), 138, 139 (br), 156, 157 (tl). **Worthing Museum & Art Gallery** 3, 11 (tr), 15 (br), 21 (bl, br), 33 (bl), 35 (tr, br), 53 (tr), 54 (bl), 55 (bl, tl), 56, 57 (tl, bl), 59 (tl, tc, bl, br), 61 (cr), 62, 63, 65 (br), 69 (tc, bl), 71 (tr), 81 (bl), 87 (br), 128, 139 (tr), 142, 145 (tr), 154.
Other individuals who kindly lent us either their own dolls or doll-associated items: Chris Dawson 126 (tl); Lucinda and Emma Ganderton 17 (tr), 89 (tl), 121 (br); Hilary Kennelly 120 (tl); exhibit on loan to Worthing

Museum by a former Worthing resident 59 (tl, tc); Carol Wagner Merriman 113 (c); Lynne and Michael Roche 81 (cl), 128; Gunilla Rosengren 101 (bl); Kevin Ryan 9 (bl), 137 (b); E.J. Taylor 30 (br), 146, 147; Matthew Ward 126.

The author and publisher also thank the **following manufacturers** for permission to reproduce their dolls in this book: A.C. Fincken, *Sunny Jim* 95 (tl); Alexander Doll Co., *Dionne Quintuplet Baby* and *Toddler Dolls*, *Dr. Allan Roy Dafoe* and *Nurse Louise de Kirilene* 26–27; Chad Valley Toys – exclusive to Woolworths', *Dwarfs* from Walt Disney's film *Snow White and the Seven Dwarfs* 99 (b); DC Comics, SUPERMAN, BATMAN and ROBIN ™ and © 1993 DC Comics. All rights reserved. Used by permission of DC Comics, 111; Johnny Gruelle's *Raggedy Ann*, copyright © Johnny B. Gruelle, Playskool/Hasbro, Inc., exclusive manufacturer 89; Hasbro International Inc., *Sindy* 120, 121 (tl, tr, bl), *Patch* 121 (c, br), *Action Man* (*G.I. Joe*, US) 126, 127 (tl); Ideal UK, 1960s *Shirley Temple* 114, 1982 *Shirley Temple* 115 (tl), 1930s *Shirley Temple* 115 (tr); Jesco, *Bisque Kewpie* 86, *Celluloid Kewpies* 104 (br). "The KEWPIE® Trademark and KEWPIE® characters are protected by U.S. Trademark and Copyright Registrations, exclusively licensed to Jesco and reprinted under permission from Jesco." Mattel UK Ltd., *Barbie* 116, 117, *Ken* 127 (bl, bc), *Heart Family* 128 (b); Merrythought Ltd., *Two Dwarfs* from Walt Disney's film *Snow White and the Seven Dwarfs* 99 (c); Villy Nielsen A/S, *Judith Mother and Baby* 129 (tc); Royal Doulton Limited, 124, 125: these items are no longer made by the Company, having been discontinued in 1985.

THE COMMISSIONED PHOTOGRAPHS

All photographs by **Matthew Ward**, except: **Lynton Gardiner** 1 (c), 3 (c), 6 (l, r), 9 (tl), 14, 15 (tl, bl), 22, 23 (c, br), 26, 27, 32, 33, 42 (br), 43, 44, 45 (except tl), 46, 47 (except br), 48, 49 (except c), 50, 51 (except tl, bl), 74 (r), 75, 88, 90, 91 (except tr), 92, 93 (except tl), 97, 99 (tr), 101 (tl, tr), 104 (br), 105 (br), 106, 107 (tr), 138 (cl), 139 (br), 156 (bl), 157 (tl); and **Tony Sandin** 101 (bl).

THE COMMISSIONED ILLUSTRATIONS

The decorative watercolor, gouache, and airbrush on paper illustrations are the work of Marc Adams.
The decorative line devices and the drawing of a hand, used to indicate doll height, are the work of Stephen Dew.

ARCHIVE PICTURE CREDITS

Ashmolean Museum, Oxford 11 (br); Bridgeman Art Library 7 (bl); by kind permission of the Chairman, Mr. Mohamed Al Fayed, Harrods Ltd./Reuters 110 (b); Ursula Gander-Bonet 53; The Hulton Picture Company 31; Japan National Tourist Organization 131 (tl); Oscar and Peter Johnson 8 (c); Maidstone Museum and Art Gallery 43; Mary Evans Picture Library 89; Retrograph Archive 104 (l); by courtesy of the Board of Trustees of the Victoria & Albert Museum 11 (tl).

NOVELTY HAT-DOFFER *The sprightly fellow waving a jaunty farewell to* The Ultimate Doll Book *is of English origin, made at the end of the 19th century. It has a ceramic head, with molded and painted hair and painted features, and wooden arms and legs. A squeeze of the bellows, which is housed inside the wire body, activates the doll's hat-doffing right arm. Ht:* 8in (20cm)